Constance Gordon Cumming

Fire Fountains

The kingdom of Hawaii, its volcanoes, and the history of its missions. Vol. 2

Constance Gordon Cumming

Fire Fountains
The kingdom of Hawaii, its volcanoes, and the history of its missions. Vol. 2

ISBN/EAN: 9783337149499

Printed in Europe, USA, Canada, Australia, Japan

Cover: Foto ©ninafisch / pixelio.de

More available books at **www.hansebooks.com**

FIRE FOUNTAINS

THE KINGDOM OF HAWAII

ITS VOLCANOES, AND THE HISTORY OF ITS MISSIONS

BY

C. F. GORDON CUMMING

AUTHOR OF 'A LADY'S CRUISE IN A FRENCH MAN-OF-WAR'
'AT HOME IN FIJI,' ETC.

IN TWO VOLS.—VOL. II.

WITH ILLUSTRATIONS AND MAPS

WILLIAM BLACKWOOD AND SONS
EDINBURGH AND LONDON
MDCCCLXXXIII

All Rights reserved

CONTENTS OF THE SECOND VOLUME.

CHAPTER XIV.

TRADE-WINDS — THE CAPITAL OF MAUI — THE LEPER SETTLEMENT — HONOLULU FORTY YEARS AGO — CHURCHES — THE ROYAL FAMILY—ALOHA, ... 1

CHAPTER XV.

HAWAII SIXTY YEARS AGO—MYTHOLOGY—THE GOD OF WAR—SACRIFICES—GODS OF THE VOLCANO—CAPTAIN COOK WORSHIPPED IN MISTAKE FOR THE EXPECTED GOD ORONO, . 17

CHAPTER XVI.

HAWAIIAN HISTORY — THE GREAT KING — THE FIRE-GODS DECLARE IN HIS FAVOUR—ABOLITION OF IDOLATRY, . . 39

CHAPTER XVII.

HAWAIIAN MORALS—DRESS—HAIR-DRESSING—COMMENCEMENT OF THE MISSION — A BLIND DANCER — KING AND QUEEN VISIT ENGLAND AND DIE — PERNICIOUS INFLUENCE OF CERTAIN FOREIGNERS, ... 74

CHAPTER XVIII.

GRADUAL WORKING OF THE CHRISTIAN LEAVEN—"THE IRON CABLE"—KAPIOLANI DEFIES THE GODDESS OF THE VOLCANO—A TIGER-LIKE CONVERT—HOW THE COLLEGE WAS BUILT—TEMPERANCE LEAGUE—BAD FOREIGN INFLUENCE—SCHOOLS FOR GIRLS, ... 115

CHAPTER XIX.

THE GREAT AWAKENING, . . 142

CHAPTER XX.

THE STORY OF HAWAII'S FOREIGN MISSIONS—THE HAWAIIAN CHURCH DECLARED INDEPENDENT OF AMERICA—PROGRESS OF MORALITY, ... 172

CHAPTER XXI.

ESTABLISHMENT OF THE ROMAN CATHOLIC MISSION—THE LAPLACE TREATY—UNJUST CLAIMS BY FRENCH AND ENGLISH SHIPS—DECLARATION OF INDEPENDENCE—THE REFORMED CATHOLIC MISSION—DEATH OF THE PRINCE OF HAWAII AND OF KAMEHAMEHA IV., . . . 190

CHAPTER XXII.

THE LAST OF THE KAMEHAMEHAS—LUNALILO THE WELL-BELOVED—HIS FUNERAL—ELECTION OF KING KALAKAUA—HIS TRAVELS—SUMMARY OF ROYAL AGE, . . 223

CHAPTER XXIII.

CONCLUSION—THE RIVER OF FIRE OF 1881—THE STORY OF A GREAT DELIVERANCE, ... 235

ILLUSTRATIONS TO THE SECOND VOLUME.

Overflow of the New Lake of Fire — In the
    Crater of Kilauea, . . *Frontispiece.*
Fire Fountains — Temporary Chimneys, *To face p.* 112
Bamboos and Bananas at Hilo,   135
Rivers of Molten Rock,   ,, 219
Map of the Hawaiian Island,   *At end.*

FIRE FOUNTAINS.

CHAPTER XIV.

TRADE-WINDS—THE CAPITAL OF MAUI—THE LEPER SETTLEMENT—HONOLULU FORTY YEARS AGO—CHURCHES—THE ROYAL FAMILY—ALOHA.

ON BOARD THE LIKE LIKE, ANCHORED OFF LAHAINA, *Saturday, 22d.*

THIS morning, after an early breakfast, the dear old father, with his own good hands, harnessed the nag, and his daughter drove me to Waikapu, by roads which had become mere channels of deep red mud.

We started early, that I might sketch the valley *en route* to the steamer; but the wind was so blustering and disagreeable, that I had to give up the attempt.

However, no one should repine at Hawaiian

gales, for I believe the extreme healthiness of these isles is attributed to the fresh pure breezes which from some quarter or other seem never to fail. For nine months of the year—from March till November—the trade-wind blows steadily from the north-east, keeping an almost uniform temperature. It is no "soft and gentle breeze," but often a very riotous and tempestuous gale—none the less healthy, however. On the larger isles its influence is modified by that of the mountains, and a sea breeze prevails by day and a land breeze at night. The land breeze, or *mamuka*, sometimes sweeps down from the mountains with such violence as to do much damage to buildings and shipping.

During the winter months the trade-winds are uncertain, calms sometimes continuing for several successive weeks, occasionally varied by a damp briny wind from the south—sometimes accompanied by heavy rain, at other times stifling, like the air from a hot stove. This is known to the Hawaiians as "the sick wind," and while it prevails, headaches, rheumatism, and influenza prevail. It is happily, however, exceptional, and during most of the winter the inhabitants can count on a cloudless sky, and a clear, dry, bracing atmosphere, which is truly invigorating.

Leaving Waikapu, we drove past the hedges of huge cactii, and the fields of tall sugar-cane with their silvery-rosy tassels, and once more stood upon the black lava-coast of Maalea Bay, where we awaited the coming of the Like Like. She has many passengers this trip, amongst others a German with a lovely voice, who has assembled an impromptu choir, chiefly of half-castes. They really have been singing beautifully.

Now we have anchored off Lahaina, which is the capital of Maui. It appears to be a very pretty little town, stretching along a white shore, with the Eka mountains rising immediately behind the settlement. I am sorry we did not arrive here earlier in the day, as it is a place of considerable interest, and of note, as one of the principal early mission stations. There is still a large seminary here, and a considerable number of foreign residents, who have made for themselves pleasant gardens and flower-bedecked homes.

A good many of the passengers have gone ashore, and I was asked to do likewise, but the inducement held out was only an indifferent travelling circus; and as it was too dark to see much of the town, I did not think it worth while.

On our way here we sighted that dreary abode of hopeless misery, the island of Molokai, to which all the lepers found in Hawaii-nei are banished for life, in the hope that by thus separating these poor afflicted ones from their fellow-creatures, this appalling disease may in time be stamped out.

For many years the leper settlement was looked upon as a sort of incurable hospital, and those who entered it were looked upon as hopelessly lost—already dead to their kindred. It is now, however, found that for some the door of hope is not altogether closed; and I learn that in the present year the Hawaiian Government has paid a sum of 20,000 dollars for the cure of lepers,—at the rate of 200 dollars (*i.e.*, £40) for each cured. So these poor sufferers have the consolation of feeling that their paternal Government watches over them with yearning pity. Indeed the King himself and Queen Kapiolani went to visit them not long ago, to prove how deeply their sympathies were touched by the sufferings of these their afflicted subjects.

Indescribably sad as is the existence of such a colony of living death, there can be no manner of doubt of the wisdom shown, first in passing, and now year by year in enforcing, a measure so necessary for the safety of this little community—not for the Hawaiian race alone, but for all who should dwell in the isles,—for the disease is as infectious as it is loathsome.

Yet the people, in their kindly carelessness, could not be induced to observe the simplest precautions. They would lie on the same mat, smoke from the same pipe, drink from the same vessel, wear the same clothes, as their friends, in all stages of the fell disease; and when at length Government interfered, and, like a wise nurse in charge of sick children, enforced a quarantine which must almost inevitably last until life's end, then they strove by every means in their power to evade this most unpopular law, and tried to hide their friends, whenever those appointed to separate the clean from the unclean were going round on their sad mission.

Nevertheless, since the commencement of the leper settlement in 1866, about fifteen hundred sufferers have been brought there year by year. Many of these, in the last stage of disease, came only to end their weary days; but some were apparently well and hearty, and their taint might have remained undiscovered for years, had they not nobly voluntarily given themselves up, for the sake of example, that others in worse plight might be the less unwilling to obey the law.

From time to time a Government mandate is issued, requiring all lepers to report themselves to the health officer of their district, and appear before him for inspection. Should he consider their symptoms to be indeed those of leprosy, he must report the case to the sheriff, who thereupon is bound to have the sufferer removed to the Isle of

Woe. To this law there is no exception. It is binding on all alike—rich and poor, gentle and simple, native and foreigner. That it is not fully carried out, is admitted on all hands, for some can always contrive to evade it; but such cases must necessarily be exceptional, and as the people are beginning to understand that the isolation of the few is the only hope of safety for the many, they now occasionally aid the Government officers in tracing out hidden cases.

The place selected for the leper settlement seems to have been very wisely chosen. It is a wide grassy plain stretching along the windward shore of Molokai, and so perfectly separated from the rest of the island by a precipitous face of crags 2000 feet in height, that there is small temptation to scale the barrier. Even communication from the sea is not easy; but thus only can provisions be obtained. So in very stormy weather, when freight and cattle cannot be landed, the community are entirely dependent for food on the Government stores, and have to do without fresh meat. The village lies at some distance from the shore, on a breezy, sunny site.

At the present time there are upwards of 800 lepers on Molokai.

These are not "lepers as white as snow." The form of the disease here prevalent is known as

Chinese leprosy, and, from the descriptions I hear (for the Hawaiian lepers are now so well separated or concealed, that I have never seen one), the symptoms are apparently the same as in the loathsome objects I have occasionally beheld in the streets of Chinese cities. Face and limbs are alike red and swollen, the features distorted, the skin shining, the eyes glassy. In advanced cases the leprosy eats away both flesh and bones; fingers and toes, hands and feet, finally whole limbs, drop off in the last stage of rottenness, and the wretched being literally dies piecemeal—truly a pitiful sight.

But terrible as is this form of the foul disease, I am told that the most fatal and infectious cases are those in which a few hard black spots appearing on the skin are the sole external symptom of the dread malady within.

While, as in duty bound, carrying out the sad law of isolation, the paternal Government and its officers have endeavoured as far as possible to lighten its woe, by making the leper village of Kalawao as much as possible like other villages, in that it has churches, schools, stores, even Government offices. There, as elsewhere, all live more or less according to their means; the poor in grass-huts such as they are accustomed to—the rich in wooden houses, with verandahs and gardens. All alike receive necessary clothing, and daily rations of good solid food; but for all superfluities they are dependent on their own resources or the gifts of friends. Various small luxuries are to be obtained at the Government store, by those who can afford to purchase them.

Of course the hospital is a very important feature, and we may be sure that in a country which takes such just pride in the admirable hospital at Honolulu, that of Molokai is not neglected. It consists of a group of twelve wooden cottages, all enclosed by a fence. Under the supervision of Dr Neilson, they are kept scrupulously clean, inside and out; indeed the appearance of those spotless whitewashed buildings seems in almost painful contrast to the loathly rottenness within.

This cottage hospital stands apart on a green hill, with pleasant lawn and shrubbery.

The present resident superintendent is Mr Clayton Strawn, a white man, who contracted the disease in Honolulu. He went to Philadelphia, where it declared itself, and he returned to the islands to end his days on Molokai. Among the recent arrivals is a poor young foreigner not twenty years of age. Imagine what a double portion of horror for a young white man to be thus consigned to this living tomb at the very opening of life!

One there is—not a leper—who, in pitying love to these outcasts, has voluntarily taken his place for life in their midst. Father Damien, a young Roman Catholic priest, resolved some years ago to devote himself to this work, and, following the Master's steps, seek and strive to save these poor sheep in the wilderness. It was a truly noble act; for, apart from the daily horror of his surroundings, there must be the ever-present knowledge that he may any day develop symptoms of the deathly doom. Hitherto, however, that devoted life has been mercifully preserved, and the good young Father continues to be a centre of brightness and sunshine in that sad colony. Two small chapels, about three miles apart, have been built by his exertions, that the feeblest members of his flock may the more readily seek rest in "the Church's shade."

The Protestant congregation is in charge of a native pastor, himself a leper (there are several such on the island); and the poor little children, born to such a heritage of woe, are taught by leper teachers in two schools.

Latterly a company of volunteers has been formed, though it is hard to imagine what pleasure these poor creatures can derive in playing at being soldiers. The very sight of them is saddening to such as behold them.

The greatest success is the leper band, for the whole community thoroughly enjoy their cheerful music, which is said to be very good. The choir, too, is excellent, and is led by a young girl with a really exquisite voice—truly a nightingale in a dreary prison.

They say, however, that even here, use becomes second nature, and that those constantly living among their hideous kind do in a measure learn to forget; that the light-hearted Hawaiian temperament triumphs, so far as almost to forget this terrible curse; and that the plain of Kalawao rings with sounds of laughter and of mirth, as joyous as those which echo through the happier valleys where disease and death are the exception—not, as here, the steadfast doom resting on all.

For that matter, the doom, not of leprosy, but of extinction, seems, alas! to overshadow the whole race, for every island has the same sad story of a population dwindling away. The valleys which a few years ago counted 4000 inhabitants, have now 400—those which had 2000 can barely muster 200. The general census, which in 1832 gave a return of 130,132, gives for last year[1] 57,985, and of these only 44,088 are Hawaiians.

HONOLULU, *Sunday Evening.*

We arrived here early this morning, and Governor Dominis brought me to this pleasant house,

[1] 1878.

which is alike the home of his mother and of Princess Liliuo-kalani, his wife. The latter occupies her own suite of apartments. Mr Dominis has commended me to the especial care of his mother —a dear old lady, stiff with rheumatism, and her hands shaking with pain; but bright and clever, and full of keen interest in life.

As we sat in her verandah looking at the lovely masses of blossom and the pleasant turf lying in cool shadow beneath large beautiful trees, she told me she remembered when there were only seven trees in the whole valley; and how she herself began to make the very first garden at Honolulu, by preparing a tiny plot before the window of her own bare wooden house, and there attempting to strike some geranium cuttings—an attempt much discouraged by her husband, who assured her that it was hopeless to think of making anything grow on such soil. The young wife was not easily daunted, however. She persevered, till her garden was a source of amazement to her few neighbours, who of course followed her good example.

Now she lives to see that region of fine cinders converted into a flourishing town, where hundreds of happy homes are embowered in beautiful flowers, and shaded by tall trees of many different species —all growing so naturally, that strangers on arriving here suppose them to be the spontaneous vegetation of these lavish tropics.

After morning service in the little English church, I had the pleasure of a few words with Bishop Willis; and afterwards called on Queen Emma, who was most kind and cordial.

In the afternoon various friends came to hear about the volcano trip; and so the time was filled up till evening service, when the choir sang "A few more years,"—a hymn which, to me, is associated with all manner of services in all manner of remote countries—from the wilds of Ross-shire to the British Legation at Pekin!

As we left the church, the lovely moonlight tempted me to a stroll with a party of friends, which was thoroughly enjoyable, the air laden with the scent of many blossoms.

It struck me that although the Episcopal church was fairly filled, the form of worship originally established by the American Congregational Mission is evidently that which finds most favour with the Hawaiians. Here the Congregationalists have four churches, at two of which the services are conducted in English, at the other two in the vernacular. Each of these has morning and evening Sunday service, and a prayer-meeting on Wednesday evenings.

The English Episcopal Church provides English

services at 6.30 and 11 A.M., and 7.30 P.M. The service is also conducted in Hawaiian at 9 A.M. and 3.30 P.M.—the Bishop, and his two assistants Mr Mackintosh and Mr Blackburn, dividing the day's work. They also hold a morning Sunday-school.

At the Roman Catholic Church, Low Mass is said daily at 6 and 7 A.M., and High Mass on Sundays and saints' days at 10 A.M. There are three services on Sunday. The Bishop (who bears the title of Bishop of Arathea) is assisted by two priests.

There is also a Christian Chinese church, where service is conducted on Sundays and Wednesday evenings by a Chinese pastor, by name Sit Moon.

ON BOARD THE S.S. AUSTRALIA,
Monday, 24th.

This morning I had a very agreeable interview with King Kalakaua and Queen Kapiolani, Mr Wodehouse having previously obtained permission to present me. He kindly called for me, and took me to the palace (rather a misnomer, as it is a very simple foreign house—probably quite as large as is necessary: it is, however, soon to be replaced by a much more extensive and palatial building). We were received by Colonel Judd. Immediately afterwards their Majesties came in and welcomed us in the most kind and unaffected way.

The King was dressed in a suit of plain black, and the Queen in very handsome black silk and velvet. She cannot speak English, but the King acted as her ready interpreter, and conversed most agreeably on various topics. They expressed a wish to see my pictures of the volcano, so a messenger was despatched to fetch the portfolio, which they examined with much interest.

When returned, it was accompanied with excellent photographs of the King and Queen with their autographs, and an immense bouquet.

Amongst his other accomplishments, King Kalakaua is an admirable musician, as is also his sister Princess Lydia. The latter composed both words and music of the National Anthem of Hawaii.

This has been a terribly busy last day. There was still so much to see, and so many kind cordial people who came to speed me on my way. Dear old Mrs Dominis invited me to remain with her till next month—and the temptation was great; but all the letters from over the sea call me "home," and the word sounds so pleasant that I have obeyed the call.[1]

[1] A grave, sentimental error, against which I would earnestly warn

Amongst the many friends who came to see me this afternoon was Queen Emma—always sweet and kind.

Then Princess Lydia drove me in her own carriage to the wharf, and gave me quaint pretty *leis* and other things made of brown seeds, by the Hawaiian women. The governor had himself seen all my luggage on board, so I had nothing to think of but to enjoy the last hour with my Honolulu friends, nearly all of whom had come to give me their last *alohas!* the most comprehensive expression of kindliness that exists in any language.

Queen Emma had sent one of her ladies as the bearer of her last words of good cheer. She was simply *laden* with flowery *leis*—one of the lovely wax-like ginger blossoms, one of white lilies, and several of other fragrant flowers,—all of which she wreathed round my neck and hat, to the wonder and envy of several of the New Zealand passengers, to whom I afterwards distributed some of my treasures; so now we are all adorned with these sweet, too short-lived memorials of kindly Hawaii.

all my friends. There can scarcely be a greater mistake than, after a long spell in the warm, green, luxurious tropics, to return to the States, or to Britain, in the cold chill of leafless winter months. The only chance of being "let down easy" is to return in the month of May at the earliest.

The sun set as we steamed out of harbour, and Honolulu looked its very best in the mellow evening light. Then came the soft clear moonlight, idealising the bare rugged coast; and now Oahu lies far behind us, and I have sadly bidden my farewell to the last of the Pacific Isles, in which I have lived for five happy years.

ALOHA! ALOHA!

CHAPTER XV.

HAWAII SIXTY YEARS AGO—MYTHOLOGY—THE GOD OF WAR—SACRIFICES—GODS OF THE VOLCANO—CAPTAIN COOK WORSHIPPED IN MISTAKE FOR THE EXPECTED GOD ORONO.

Is it not strange to think of these truly dignified queens and princesses holding court receptions at which they and their ladies of honour appear in low-necked, short-sleeved dresses of richest material, and latest Parisian-American fashion, and then to remember that it is only exactly one hundred years since Tiha, the king of Kauai, sent to Poriorani, king of Oahu, a priceless gift—namely, a yard and a half of common canvas, which had been obtained from Captain Cook's ship, by a man rejoicing in the name of Aamo, "skin of a lizard's egg"?

As in duty bound, Poriorani presented this treasure to Opuhani, his queen, who wore it as her court train, and was the admired of all beholders. The precious fabric was named Aamo, to do honour to the man who had procured it from the floating city.

Still more difficult is it, in presence of this highly organised Christian community, to realise that it is just sixty-two years since the very first Christian teacher set foot on these isles; and that, previous to the year 1819, the people of Hawaii were worshippers of all manner of strange gods, to whom they offered even human sacrifice. Such were Keoroeva and Tairi, national war-gods, which were carried to battle by their priests to insure victory.

These gods were no light burden, being great blocks of wood several feet high, with heads and necks formed of fine wickerwork, covered with red feathers so curiously wrought as to resemble the skin of a bird. The face was hideous, having a mouth from ear to ear, armed with triple rows of shark's teeth, and eyes of mother-of-pearl. The head was adorned with long tresses of human hair, and crowned with a shapely feather helmet. The priests who carried these repulsive deities uttered terrific yells, and distorted their own countenance, the better to encourage their own warriors, and alarm the foe.

The great King Kamehameha had a tutelary god which he held in such reverence that it accompanied him everywhere, and was always placed under his pillow when he slept. It could not have been a pleasant bedfellow, being a rudely hewn block of wood, so poisonous that several of the men who cut it, with their short-handled stone adzes, died from its malignant influence. Then it was miraculously revealed to the survivors that they must cover their faces and bodies with dracæna-leaves, and cloth of bark-fibre, and, only leaving one small opening for one eye, might carve the image with their daggers. So the idol was made, and called Karai-pahoa—*i.e.*, the dagger-carved—and for many generations he was worshipped as the lord of all poisons.

But far more popular were the great stone images of Raeapua and Kaneapua, the sea-gods, to whom the fishermen made their petitions, that the shoals of fishes might be directed to their shores. Chief among the marine gods was Moo-alii, the king of sharks—himself a shark—to whom temples were erected on every jutting headland, more especially on the island of Molokai. To these, the fisher-folk carried the first-fruits of their annual harvest of the sea, as the seasons brought successive shoals of divers kinds of fish.

They even offered their own dead relations to the hungry sharks, under the belief that the spirit of their kinsmen would pass into the shark who ate him, and would thereafter incline the whole army of voracious monsters to spare such fishers as might be thrown on their mercy. So the fisher-folk wrapped their dead in sacred red cloth, and threw them into the sea to be devoured.

The fishers were also devout worshippers of various storm-gods and wind-gods, to whom they looked for help in time of dangers, and at whose altars they never failed to pay whatsoever they had vowed, so soon as they were restored in safety to the land.

The Hawaiian Esculapius was a deified herbalist of the name of Koreamoku, who had been instructed by the gods themselves in all secrets of medicinal plants and their uses. Offerings on behalf of the sick were presented before his wooden image, in the great temple at Kailua, and to him were addressed prayers for their recovery. Two of his disciples, Orono-puha and Makanui-airomo, also received divine honours, their aid being chiefly sought by such as believed themselves to be afflicted by evil spirits.

Multitudes of human victims were sacrificed on the altars of these gods on all important occasions, such as the death of a chief or a declaration of war. Thus, when Umi, the king of Hawaii, returned victorious from battle, he proceeded to offer several victims; but the priest being in a bloodthirsty mood, proved insatiable, and in the name of his god cried for more and more victims; so the king had to give up one after another of his own brave followers, till eighty corpses lay heaped before the hideous idol, and the king remained alone with the priest.

Of course, as a general rule, the victims were prisoners of war, or criminals who had infringed some of the arbitrary laws of *tabu;* moreover, a smaller number of human beings sufficed. Thus, when Kamehameha had built a great *heiau* in honour of his war-god Tairi (which was a large wooden idol covered with red feathers), he consecrated it with the usual ceremonies. Eleven men were slain on the altar, and hogs and dogs without number.

In all heathen faiths we invariably find some custom which seems to suggest a link to the old law of Moses; and, abominable as it would sound to Jewish ears to speak of the *puaa-hea,* or "hog to be entirely consumed," in the same breath with that paschal lamb of which "nothing must remain until the morning," it is impossible to hear of one without thinking of the other. The Hawaiian had neither lamb nor bullock, but he freely sacrificed the best treasures he possessed; and, so far from deeming a hog unclean, it was generally a family pet, loved and cherished. So the great herd of swine immolated at high festivals represented many a true individual sacrifice.

At the consecration of a temple, profound silence

was enjoined for many hours on several successive days, while the priests, with arms stretched heavenward, united in prayers and chants. On the eighth day of the dedication, the *puaa-hea* was sacrificed, and all present were required to taste of that meat, that it might be consumed to the uttermost fragment; for should any portion of it remain, it was believed that some terrible calamity would ensue, and that all the worshippers would perish.

A large and very influential body of priests were devoted to the service of the temples. Their office was hereditary, and secured many privileges. They owned much land, and the people living on their estates were virtually their slaves. Each priestly family was, by inheritance, devoted to the service of some special god, and could not officiate at the temple of any other deity. The king alone had free access to the most sacred enclosure, of all temples alike. The priest in charge of the national war-god was recognised as the great high priest of Hawaii.

There was only one really distinctive feature in the Hawaiian Pantheon—namely, the fire-loving gods of the volcanoes, a mighty and numerous family, who were worshipped in fear and trembling. The supreme ruler in the house of fire was the goddess Pélé (a short name, easy to remember, which accordingly quickly becomes familiar to every traveller in Hawaii). Her relations had longer names, and are therefore forgotten. Amongst them were two deformed brothers—*Ke-oahi-kama-kaua*, "the fire-thrusting child of war," and *Ka-poha-ikahi-ola*, "the explosion in the palace of life."

Two more brothers were *Ke-ua-ke-po*, "the rain of night," and *Kane-kekili*, the thundering god. There were several sisters. *Makole-wawa-hi-waa* was "the fiery-eyed canoe-breaker." She dwelt in the surging billows of that fiery lake whereon never a canoe floated. And when the dark cloud above the crater reflected the red glow of the fire fountains beneath, the Hawaiians whispered a word of prayer to *Hiaka-wawahi-lani*, "the cloud-ruler who dwells in heaven."

Besides these, a multitude of Pélé's kinsfolk dwelt in her fire-palaces. All were malignant spirits, exerting their power only for evil, and delighting in deeds of vengeance and destruction, in causing earthquakes, or pouring lava-floods on the fertile lands. Consequently they were held in the deepest awe, and no pains were spared to propitiate them. On the first alarm of an eruption, whole herds of swine, both alive, and already cooked, were thrown into the crater, with many another precious offering, to secure the goodwill of these mischievous rulers of the infernal regions.

A curious legend tells how Pélé was wooed by Kama-puaa, the great centaur of Hawaii—a gigantic monster, half man, half hog. Pélé rejected his addresses, and took refuge inside the volcano; but the demi-hog followed, and poured floods of water down the chimney of the crater, hoping to bring her to the surface. But her fiery subjects licked up the water-floods, and rushed out upon the monster in columns of steam, pursuing him even to the sea with showers of fire and stones.

With the exception of these unique volcanic gods, the old mythology[1] of Hawaii appears to have been almost identical with that of Tahiti. The early missionaries who came here from the Society Islands found a very marked similarity in all their legends and customs. There were the same "feather gods," who were worshipped with similar set forms of prayer and chanting—the same *etus* or *totems* (*i.e.*, living creatures, fish, birds, and insects, in whom the gods were supposed to dwell) —notably the shark and the kingfisher. Captain King has recorded the reverence paid to two tame ravens, which were shown to him by the villagers as their *etu*.

But even at the date of Captain Cook's arrival in

---

[1] For mythology of Tahiti, see 'A Lady's Cruise in a French Man-of-War' (by C. F. Gordon Cumming), vol. ii. p. 189.

the Isles,[1] he noticed that though sacrifices were offered and litanies chanted to the gods, the idols were treated with scant reverence. In fact, the Hawaiians were at that time watching for the return to earth of their deified king, Orono, who, at his coming, should supersede the lesser gods. Hence it was that, on the arrival of Kapena Kuke (as they afterwards called Captain Cook), they assumed that he must be their expected god, and so rendered him homage which was literally adoration—an error which he most unfortunately saw fit to encourage.

It is the fashion in all books of travel to observe that every schoolboy knows all about Captain Cook. Now, I never was a schoolboy; and it is so many years since my worthy old Swiss *bonne* used to describe me as "*un Tom, et puis, un romping boy*"—which, I suppose, was the equivalent of a Tom-boy or schoolboy—that I had forgotten the details of this old story; so it was with great delight that I hailed the little old-fashioned series of many volumes, bound in brown leather, and read it once more.

As you likewise have probably forgotten it, I may as well remind you how, on the arrival of the

[1] Cook landed in Kealakeakua Bay, in the Isle of Hawaii, on January 17, 1779.

ships, all the people of Hawaii flocked to the shore to see the mighty canoe in which their divine king had returned to his kingdom. So great a multitude assembled, that fully three thousand canoes were lying in the bay; and whenever Cook landed, the people prostrated themselves on the ground in deepest humility, covering their faces, and only rising when he had passed. Then they crowded after him in a crouching attitude, literally almost like dogs, running on hands and knees to keep as near him as possible. This crowd numbered about fifteen thousand persons!

Whenever the Hawaiian chiefs or priests, or even the king himself, approached Captain Cook, they invariably brought the accustomed temple offering of a small pig, which they laid at his feet, and a piece of red cloth, which, with every mark of veneration, they threw over his shoulders, while reciting certain formulas or prayers, in which the word Orono[1] frequently occurred. The strangers soon discovered that Orono was the name of an invisible being, who was supposed to dwell in the heavens. They also noticed that the idols in the temples, and they only, were always arrayed in

---

[1] O-Rono. The name was really Lono, with the honorific O, which Captain Cook very naturally supposed to form part of the word. Hence he speaks of O-Whyee (Hawaii), and O-Taheiti, (Tahiti). He also frequently uses *r* in place of *l*, as in Honoruru, for Honolulu.

sacred red cloth, and that small pigs were generally laid on the altars, and there left to putrefy. The similarity of the forms of invocation addressed to the gods, and to the new-comers, was also noted.

Nevertheless, this worship was freely allowed; and Captain King has recorded how, one day when Captain Cook went ashore, the people as usual fell prostrate before him, with their faces to the ground, while officials bearing wands, tipped with dog's hair, went before him, heralding the approach of Orono. They led him to the sacred *heiau*, which was a great platform, 40 yards long by 20 broad, and 14 in height. The top was surrounded by a wooden rail, ornamented with skulls of the victims who had there been slain in sacrifice.

Captain Cook was first led up and formally presented to two large wooden images of repulsive ugliness. They were swathed in red cloth, and to them the priests chanted litanies. At the other end of the *heiau* stood twelve images ranged in a semicircle, and one central idol, wrapped in red cloth, and having before it an altar covered with divers fruits, on which was laid a putrid hog. The latter most unsavoury offering was unceremoniously appropriated by the chief priest, who held it towards Cook while reciting a long speech.

At one side of the *heiau* was an irregular sort of scaffolding, supported on five poles, upwards of 20 feet high. To this very undesirable eminence Cook was now requested to climb, which he did, not without great risk of falling. At that moment ten men approached, bearing a live hog and a large piece of red cloth. They prostrated themselves, while the chief priest proceeded to wrap the red cloth round him whom they desired to honour, but who sat very awkwardly perched aloft, with difficulty keeping his place among the rotten scaffolding, while the priests chanted a long litany, partly in alternate sentences, and partly in concert, while offering him the live hog.

At length the honoured representative of Orono was allowed to descend from his perilous position, and was led back to the twelve images, to each of whom the warrior-priest, Koah, addressed some sneering remark, snapping his fingers at them in a most irreverent fashion. But he prostrated himself before the central figure, and kissed it, bidding the new deity do likewise, which he accordingly did.

They next proceeded to a sort of sunken temple, into which they descended, and Cook was seated between two wooden idols, while Koah supported one of his arms, and bade Captain King uphold the other. A second procession of natives then brought a feast, consisting of a baked hog, puddings, and vegetables. This was also offered in due form, while priests and people chanted a litany, with regular responses, all addressed to Orono.

The noxious drink of the Pacific, which is here called *ava*,[1] was then prepared in the usual manner by chewing the root. But exceptional horrors were in store for the honoured guest. First one of the priests chewed the kernel of a cocoa-nut, and therewith anointed the face, head, hands, arms, and shoulders of the long-suffering stranger, while the dreadful old chief, who had handled the putrid hog, proceeded to pull the flesh from off the baked hog, and put pieces in the mouth of the stranger; and, remarking that he could not manage to swallow one morsel, the polite old man proceeded to chew select portions for his benefit!

After this very trying ceremony, the mysterious strangers returned to their ship, remarking, as before, that, as they passed along the beach, preceded by the official herald of Orono, the people either retired or fell prostrate on the shore.

This sort of reception does not appear to have in any way shocked the great navigator; for when, a few days later, he learnt that the priests lived together in a secluded village, he determined to visit them, and took his artist to make a drawing of the ceremony, which, he fully expected, would be repeated.

[1] Kava, or Yangona.

Nor was he disappointed. He was at once conducted to the Harre-no-Orono—*i.e.*, the house of Orono—and seated at the foot of a wooden idol. Again Captain King was desired to uphold one of his arms, while a priest upheld the other. Again he was wrapped in red cloth, while a company of thirteen priests offered him a live pig, with the usual ceremonies. They then strangled and singed it in the wood-fire, and held it under Captain Cook's nose, while chanting their litanies. Finally, a fat hog, ready dressed, was brought in, and the guests were fed, as before.

Thenceforth, whenever this representative of deity moved, he was attended by one of these priests, who preceded him, announcing the coming of Orono, and bidding the people prostrate themselves. The same watchful herald accompanied him when on the water, standing at the bow of the boat, with his wand of office, to announce his approach to any natives they might meet. These instantly ceased paddling their canoes, and lay down on their faces till he had passed. Ere long the king, Kalaniopuu (whom Cook calls Terreeoboo), came in person to do homage to his supposed lord.

Accompanied by two other chiefs, dressed in rich feathered cloaks and helmets, and armed with long spears and daggers, they left the village in a large canoe, followed by a second, in which were a party of priests, with their idols, displayed on red cloth. These were "busts of a gigantic size, made of wickerwork, and curiously covered with small feathers of various colours, wrought in the same manner as their cloaks. Their eyes were made of large pearl-oysters, with a black nut fixed in the centre; their mouths were set with a double row of the fangs of dogs, and strangely distorted. A third boat was filled with hogs and vegetables."

This procession paddled round the ship, while the priests sang their hymns with great solemnity. They then returned to shore, where Captain Cook followed them. The king rose to meet him, and gracefully threw over him his own royal feather cloak, placed a feathered helmet on his head, and a curious fan in his hand. Further, he spread at his feet half-a-dozen beautiful large cloaks, of inestimable value in the eyes of a Hawaiian.

In return for these priceless gifts from the brown king, the white man presented him with one white shirt and his own hanger. Certainly, by their own showing, these early navigators gave small equivalent for the hospitality lavished on them by the poor but generous islanders, while their peccadilloes in the way of pilfering were severely dealt with. Some were fired at with small-shot, and one was carried on board and flogged.

Ere long, the faith of the people in the divinity

of their guests was considerably shaken by the death of one of the sailors, whose body was carried ashore for burial.

Furthermore, a most rude shock to their feelings of veneration was given when,[1] the vessel being in need of fuel and of timber for repairs, Cook bade Captain King purchase the railing which surmounted the sacred *heiau*, its posts consisting of rudely carved idols. The purchase-money offered was two iron hatchets. The offer was indignantly refused; whereupon the sailors received orders to break down the fence and carry it to the boats, which they proceeded to do, while priests and chiefs looked on in speechless horror, not venturing to contradict the orders of Orono, but somewhat shaken in their faith. To avoid the appearance of taking the fence by force, the two hatchets were thrust into the folds of the high priest's garment, whence they were removed by an attendant, the priest not condescending to notice such rude payment. Meanwhile the people had gathered round, much incensed, and endeavoured to replace the fence and images, which, however, were finally carried on board.[2]

This act of desecration tended greatly to turn the tide of popular feeling; and when, a few days later,

---

[1] On the 2d February.

[2] See the account given by Lieutenant Ledyard, who was one of the party told off for the removal of the fence.

a party came ashore to repair the rudder of one of the ships, the natives showed less readiness than usual to assist them. The white men struck the brown, the latter threw stones — a general fray ensued, which ended in the sailors and marines discreetly retiring.

But the chief cause for the revulsion of feeling lay in the very serious expense of entertaining so many flesh-consuming demi-gods (even if they *were* gods, which now appeared doubtful). The sacrifices required for the idols were comparatively few; but these desired daily offerings on so large a scale, that the natives, whose own supplies were not overabundant, began to dread a famine.

Already had the two large vessels[1] lain in harbour for a fortnight, and their requisitions, both for present and future use, weighed so heavily on the people, that, when the explorers prepared to seek fresh pastures, their departure was hailed even more gladly than had been their coming. At the command of their chief, the natives prepared a great farewell gift of food and cloth—an offering of large value, which was carried on board, without any return being made; though some fireworks were let off to astonish the savages, who, supposing them to be flying devils, were greatly alarmed by the display.

[1] The Discovery and the Resolute.

On the 4th February, the vessels weighed anchor, but were becalmed within sight of land for two days, when the hospitable king sent off canoes laden with fresh provisions of hogs and vegetables. At length a breeze sprang up, and carried the ships out of sight, greatly to the satisfaction of the people. The breeze freshened to a gale. The Resolute sprang her foremast; and, to the dismay of the Hawaiians, both vessels returned to their anchorage within a week of the day on which they had sailed.

Then all was changed. Instead of feasting, singing, and dancing, troubles thickened on every hand. The constant infringement of the *tabus* kept up a perpetual irritation—quarrels and disputes became almost continuous. Finally, one of the ship's boats was stolen, and on the following morning (Sunday, 14th) Cook went to the house of the king, and tried to induce him to come on board, intending to keep him as a hostage. This was prevented by all the chiefs. Then commenced the fatal affray in which the great commander lost his life.

Even then, some of his late worshippers still maintained that he was indeed the divine Orono, and that he would one day reappear alive. His body was treated with the highest respect that could be shown to the remains of a great chief— that is to say, it was carried to a temple, where the bones were separated from the flesh, rubbed with salt, and carefully preserved.

When, after much negotiation, Captain King induced the chiefs to restore the remains, they were brought to him wrapped in a large quantity of fine new cloth, and covered with a spotted cloak of black and white feathers. They were brought with great solemnity by a high chief, robed in the long feather cloak which was only worn on great State occasions. A portion of the body had previously been brought on board by a chief, who inquired with the greatest earnestness "when the Orono would come again, and what he would do to them on his return?"

When the parcel was examined, it was ascertained that the ribs and breast-bone were missing, also the lower jaw and the feet. These were said to have burnt with the flesh; but it was afterwards ascertained that they had been conveyed to a temple of Orono on the opposite side of the isle, and were there preserved in a wicker-shrine, covered with precious red feathers, and not only received adoration from all who visited the temple, but were annually carried in procession to several other *heiaus*, and sometimes carried round the isle by the priests, when collecting offerings for the support of the temple.

On the arrival of the missionaries in 1822, great

efforts were made to recover these relics; but, though none denied that they had been thus worshipped, it was impossible to discover their fate, as chiefs and priests alike shrank from any allusion to the circumstances of Cook's unhappy fate. It was, however, supposed that, on the abolition of idolatry in 1819, they had (according to the custom observed with respect to the bones of kings and chiefs) been secretly committed to the care of some chief or priest, to be deposited in a cave known only to himself.

The hair was in the possession of the great Kamehameha; but the heart was eaten by some children, who had mistaken it for that of a dog. The names of the children are preserved in Hawaiian history. They were Kupa, Mohoole, and Kaiwikokoole. Some of the sad relics are said to have been recovered, and carried to England by King Liho Liho, to be presented to the widow of Captain Cook. The bodies of the marines who fell with him were burnt, with the exception of the principal bones, which were distributed among the chiefs.

According to Hawaiian legend, the deified Orono was one of the prehistoric kings, who in a fit of anger murdered his wife, and afterwards grieved so sorely for her death that he lost his reason, and travelled from isle to isle, boxing and wrestling with every one he met. Finally, he embarked in a canoe of strange form, and sailed away to some foreign land, whence it was supposed that he would some day return.

It was in his honour that boxing and wrestling were invested with a certain sanctity, and annually practised at his principal temples. But it is curious that these games should also have been reserved for religious festivals in Tahiti, as they still are in Japan.[1]

Captain King frequently comments on the inferior skill and prowess shown by the Hawaiians in these and other games and feats, as compared with the Tahitians, though it is difficult to assign any cause for the difference, these men being as finely built and as supple-jointed as their southern brethren—and moreover, in those days, equally unencumbered with raiment.

Captain King's summary of the characteristics of these islanders is remarkable. He says: "The Hawaiians are of the most mild and affectionate disposition, equally remote from the extreme

[1] How strange is this symbolic religious wrestling, which we trace in so many faiths, even in that of Judea! St Paul says, "We wrestle not against flesh and blood." But in that mysterious night when Jacob wrestled with the Angel of the Covenant, until the breaking of the day (Gen. xxxii. 24), and gained the name of Israel, Prince of God, the shrunken sinew remained, as an ever-enduring proof that his wrestling had been no vision, but a struggle with a tangible opponent.

levity and fickleness of the Otaheiteans, and the distant gravity and reserve of the inhabitants of the Friendly Isles. They appear to live in the utmost harmony and friendship with one another."

The estimate thus early made has certainly been proved true by all subsequent experience.

CHAPTER XVI.

HAWAIIAN HISTORY — THE GREAT KING — THE FIRE-GODS DECLARE IN HIS FAVOUR — ABOLITION OF IDOLATRY.

AMONG the chiefs who were foremost in welcoming Cook was the great warrior-king, Kamehameha, who at that time was merely the chief of Halaua and Kona, districts in Hawaii. He, however, strengthened his position by marrying Keopuolani, the highest chiefess in the isles, granddaughter to King Kalaniopau, and so a lineal descendant of the ancient kings of Maui and Hawaii.

Captain King described Kamehameha as a savage of most sternly ferocious appearance; but in later years he proved himself to be in every respect a great and noble character, of wonderful ability — brave, resolute, ambitious, yet humane, hospitable, and generous — in stature herculean, in carriage majestic, with dark piercing eyes, which seemed to penetrate the innermost thoughts of all around him, and before whose glance the most courageous quailed.

Hawaii was at that time torn by intertribal warfare—every chief seeking his own aggrandisement at the expense of his neighbours. By his genius and indomitable will, Kamehameha gradually extended his dominions, till his supremacy was acknowledged throughout Hawaii, where he strove to establish kindly relations with such foreign ships as chanced to call.

This was by no means an easy matter, for the majority of the white men who visited the isles were little better than pirates, to whom no action seemed too base or cruel, if it could serve their selfish greed of gain. Among the vessels which thus attained to evil notoriety was the American scow Eleanor, commanded by a man of the name of Metcalf. She arrived off Hawaii in the autumn of 1789, and remained there till the following spring, attended by the Fair American, a small schooner of only 26 tons, manned by five seamen, and commanded by Metcalf's son, a lad of eighteen.

After some months, the Eleanor sailed to Maui, and in the night one of her boats was stolen, and the watchman, who had fallen asleep, was murdered. In revenge, Metcalf attacked the village, killing and wounding various men, and then discovered that the thieves came from another district. He proceeded thither, and offered a reward for the remains of the seaman and the boat. These were given up, and the people innocently assembled to claim the reward, and to trade with the big ship.

When a multitude had assembled, he directed them to arrange all their canoes in order on the starboard side, which they most unsuspiciously did. Then, unveiling his battery, he poured volley after volley of musket-balls and nails into their thickest ranks, killing upwards of a hundred, and wounding many more.

Having thus revenged himself on the innocent, he returned to Hawaii, where a most just but awful retribution awaited him. The schooner Fair American, commanded by his son, got separated from the Eleanor, and arrived alone off Kawaihae Bay. The high chief of this district had for some trifling cause been severely flogged by the elder Metcalf, and now saw his opportunity for vengeance. Accordingly, he proceeded with a number of his followers to board the ship, ostensibly bearing presents. Suddenly, seizing young Metcalf, he threw him overboard, and the massacre of the seamen was quickly accomplished, only the mate being allowed to survive, though frightfully wounded.

This man, Isaac Davis, became noted in the

history of the isles. At the same time, the boatswain of the Eleanor, John Young, had gone ashore at Kealakeakua, and, to his surprise, was detained by order of the king, who (fearing another massacre, should Metcalf discover the fate of his son) had forbidden any canoe to leave the shore.

Kamehameha was sorely displeased by this act of treachery—so contrary to his own policy. Indeed, not long before, he had discovered his own people arranging a plot by which to seize the larger vessel, for his use—a plot which had every promise of success; but he at once peremptorily forbade its execution—an act of justice ill requited by the master of the vessel.

For two days the vessel lay off the bay, waiting for Young's return, and finally sailed, ignorant of what had befallen the schooner.

Young and Davis were at once taken under the personal protection of the king. These two men, though merely rough-and-ready seamen, appear to have been of a type considerably above the average, both in moral character and uprightness of purpose. Other white men had settled on the isles, mostly runaways from ships, and of very low character. The natives very quickly perceived the superiority of Young and Davis, who soon acquired great influence with the king, as faithful servants and wise counsellors. He bestowed on them valuable estates, and ere long both were treated as chiefs. Young, in particular, soon acquired so much power as to excite the jealousy of the subordinate chiefs, and especially of the priests—one of whom determined to accomplish his death by witchcraft. It was a simple process, but one which so acted on the superstitions of the people as often to accomplish its own end.

The priest built a hut in the forest, and there shut himself up, till, by his prayers and incantations, he should have accomplished the death of the doomed victim. But the white man, having been warned by the friendly king of the evil that was plotting, met the priest with his own weapons. He too built a leaf-hut in the forest, and announced that he was about to bewitch his enemy; and so well did superstitious fear do its work, that the sorcerer drooped and died, and the fame of Young increased.

Both he and Davis had by this time so won the hearts of the people, that the idea of their ever wishing to return to their own homes was intolerable. Consequently they were jealously guarded whenever a vessel appeared in sight, and were never allowed to enter a canoe: any one detected in carrying any message for them to a ship would have been put to death.

Thus they lived in honourable captivity till they

were altogether reconciled to their lot, and played a really important part as pioneers of civilisation, being the first white men of average worth with whom the Hawaiians had come in contact. Eventually Young was made the governor of the great isle of Hawaii, and acquitted himself of his duties in that high office to the satisfaction of the king, the people, and the foreign residents—whence we may infer that he possessed considerable tact. He married a high chiefess: consequently, as rank descends from the mother, his children possessed blue blood; and through her, his grand-daughter, Queen Emma Kaleleonalani (widow of Kamehameha IV.), traces her descent from the ancient royal family of Hawaii.

Two years after the affair of the Eleanor, Vancouver, who had previously served under Captain Cook, returned to Hawaii in the Discovery, and anchored in Kealakeakua Bay.[1] He brought presents of sheep, cattle, poultry, and garden-seeds, which he distributed among the people. He induced the king to place a *tabu* on the cattle, that none might be destroyed for ten years. This was faithfully carried out, though the cattle increased so rapidly, and became so wild, as to prove troublesome neighbours. From these are descended the wild herds which still roam in the forests. Van-

[1] March 3, 1792.

couver also brought gifts of many useful things, such as agricultural and carpenter's tools.

As he moved about the group, he was painfully struck by the rapid depopulation during the fourteen years which had elapsed since his previous visit. In one district he reckoned the population at one-third of its former number, and of all the chiefs with whom he had been acquainted, Kamchamcha alone survived.

The latter at once came on board, bringing John Young as his interpreter. The king was clothed in a magnificent feather cloak, which trailed upon the ground, and on his head a feather helmet. He looked every inch a king, but must have lost much of his dignity when he donned a scarlet coat, trimmed with gold-lace, presented to him by Vancouver. Taking his hand, he asked if the King of Great Britain was friendly to him, and the answer being favourable, he saluted him by touching noses.

He provided ninety large hogs, and a prodigious quantity of vegetables and fruit, for the use of the crew, and for King George he presented the most valuable article in Hawaii—namely, his own war-coat, pierced with spear-holes, with the injunction that, as it had been worn by no one but himself, none save the king of England must venture to put it on.

The warrior-king provided a characteristic cutertainment for his guests, in a sham-fight between three bodies of his most distinguished braves. They were armed with blunted spears, the king himself excelling in the art of parrying these. Six were hurled at him at once, two were parried, three he caught, and the sixth was avoided by a rapid movement. When one party had gained the victory, those who represented the slain were dragged by the heels over the beach to be first offered to the king, and then to the *heiau*, where they underwent a feigned sacrifice. On the whole, I think it can hardly have been an agreeable part to act!

Still less pleasant was the king's own part in the Makahiki, or New-Year festival, which was a sort of saturnalia generally kept up for about a month, during which the people amused themselves with dances, games, sham-fights, and theatrical performances. The festival was always commenced by the highest chief present, who, dressing himself in his rich feather armour, started at dawn in his canoe, and coasted the shore till sunrise, when he was obliged to land. The most expert of his warriors was on the watch; and as the canoe touched the beach, it was his part to throw three heavy spears at its inmate, in quick succession, from a distance of thirty paces.

These were not spears blunted for sham-fights, but the genuine article, any one of which would have killed or severely wounded their victim had he failed to turn them aside. The triumph of skill lay in catching the first spear in the hand, and with it warding off the others; the ceremony concluded with carrying the spear, point downwards, to the *heiau*, the festival being considered religious.

In after-years Kamehameha was urged to abolish a custom so dangerous to himself, but he replied that "he was as competent to catch a spear as any man was to throw one."

Mr Ellis described the skill of the Hawaiians in javelin-practice as altogether wonderful. He tells of other warriors who, like their king, would stand up and allow six men simultaneously to throw their javelins at them; these they would either catch and return on their assailants, or so dexterously turn aside that they fell harmless to the ground.

He speaks of having frequently seen seven or eight thousand persons assembled to witness the simplest native games, such as trials of skill in throwing darts and javelins, or polished stones— all of which were made to glide along a carefully prepared floor. Each isle had its champion player, who occasionally challenged the favourite of any other isle; and men, women, and children assembled in crowds, not merely as spectators, but to do their part by backing their own man, and wild betting ensued. Women staked their ornaments, and men whatever they possessed—their weapons, their tools, even the mats on which they slept. Should their champion lose the game, their anger and excitement were often so great that they would tear their hair in frantic rage.

During his stay in the isles, Vancouver strove by every means in his power to do good and to promote peace, and in every way to encourage all that tended to the welfare of the people. So thoroughly did he win their confidence, that the bad impressions left by Captain Cook's unfortunate visit were entirely done away, and the chiefs of Hawaii assembled in council and determined formally to place themselves under the protection of Great Britain. *They distinctly reserved to themselves the right of sovereignty and the entire regulation of their own domestic concerns;* nevertheless, the act was interpreted by Vancouver as a distinct act of cession of the great isle of Owhyhee to his Britannic Majesty. The English colours were hoisted, the isle was accepted in King George's name, and an inscription on copper to that effect was left in the house of Kamehameha. This misinterpretation subsequently led to serious difficulties.

Vancouver vainly endeavoured to induce the hostile chiefs to forego their animosities, and live in peace. Equally vain were his efforts to prove the foolishness of idolatry and of the oppressive system of *tabus*, and to teach the chiefs something of the nature of his own faith. He offered to send them teachers from England, should they wish to hear more concerning the true religion. His words, however, seem to have had as little effect with regard to religion as to peace. Kamehameha was determined to carry out his course of victory till he remained sole ruler in the whole group; and as the gods were supposed to be favourable to him, and the influence of the priests valuable, this union of Church and State was not to be trifled with.

He had good reason to encourage the popular belief in the supernatural aid granted to him by favouring deities; for on one occasion, in the early days of his career, he was sorely harassed by simultaneous wars in Maui and on Hawaii, which compelled him to go in person to the former, leaving Kiana, a friendly chief, to take command of his warriors in Hawaii.

The contest would have been of very doubtful issue had not the mighty Pélé, goddess of the great volcano, interposed in favour of the young chief.

As the enemy, commanded by Keoua, were marching across the isle from Hilo to Ka-u to attack the forces of Kamehameha, they had to encamp in the neighbourhood of the volcano, when a terrific storm of thunder and lightning commenced. Supernatural darkness overspread earth and heaven, weird red and blue lights flashed in awful glare from the crater, and the earth rocked so appallingly that the stoutest hearts quailed, and none dared to move from his place lest the next step should precipitate him into some yawning chasm.

For two days and nights Keoua and his tribe halted, terror-stricken. Then, having to choose between starvation and movement, they determined to advance. In order to divide the danger, they separated into three companies, and started at intervals. The first company had gone but a little way when a violent earthquake shook the ground, so that they reeled to and fro like drunken men, unable to stand still or to proceed. Then great Pélé unmasked her batteries, and, with a roar far exceeding the loudest thunder-crash, pursued them with such a volley of artillery that the miracle seems that any could have escaped. The sky, which but a moment before had been unclouded, was filled with a shower of cinders and ashes, extending for many miles around, while the air was poisoned with sulphureous gases. The ashes were thrown to so great a height that they were partly cooled in their descent; and so the majority of the first company were uninjured, only a few of their number being overwhelmed and suffocated.

At the appointed interval the second party

started, and then in due time the third. The latter experienced much the same dangers as the first detachment, but hurried onwards, and escaped with little loss.

But what was their consternation on discovering their comrades of the central division lying stark and dead! Four hundred human beings, with their wives and their little ones, lay as if in sleep, stifled by the sulphureous vapours. Some were sitting upright, with their families grouped around them in close embrace; others lying down, apparently in natural sleep. It was like the destruction of the Assyrians, when

> "The Angel of Death spread his wings on the blast,
> And breathed on the face of the foe as he passed."

Death must have been instantaneous; and the only creature that had survived was a hog (probably one of the usual Hawaiian family pets, which are often more cherished than the children). This creature was quietly and unconcernedly hunting about for food.

Probably the action of sulphur tended to preserve the bodies, for they remained unchanged and uncorrupted for many days. Finally, the flesh dropped from the bones, which were left to bleach in the sun—a warning to all men of the fate awaiting whosoever should venture to fight against the favourite of the gods.

This is the first eruption of the volcano of Kilauea of which there is any record. It appears to have differed from all those of more recent date, in that no lava-stream is mentioned—only sand and scoria, with volumes of steam and sulphureous vapour. It appears to have been of precisely the same character as the eruption of Vesuvius, A.D. 79, when Pompeii and Herculaneum were overwhelmed.

It stands to reason that, with so simple and superstitious a race as the Hawaiians, Pélé's intervention on behalf of Kamehameha carried great weight, and lent an almost magic power to his arms — an obligation which the king was ever ready to acknowledge: so to his last hour he vigorously upheld the whole system of idolatry and the power of the priests, who, on their side, did not fail to support such a devout and powerful worshipper.

So the great chief pursued his career of conquest, till, to his original patrimony on Hawaii, he had added the whole of that isle, and then passed on to Maui, Lanai, Molokai, Oahu, and even Kauai, the wildest and most remote of all. Thus he had accomplished his heart's desire, and reigned supreme throughout Hawaii-nei (the name by which the group collectively is called).

Then, when there remained no more foes to conquer, this energetic king had leisure to show his true greatness by the exceeding wisdom with which he ruled his dominions. By a clemency hitherto unknown in native warfare, he won the affections of the vanquished, who became his most devoted servants.

The prolonged intertribal wars had reduced the country to a condition of abject misery. Fighting, famine, pestilence, and oppression had combined to depopulate the group. On the isle of Oahu, provisions were so scarce that many natives had died of starvation. Others had been burnt alive by their own chiefs for stealing food to supply their famishing families. Now the days of ruthless oppression were at an end. Kamehameha put down crime with a high hand. He enacted laws prohibiting murder, theft, and oppression, and appointed governors in every isle, and officers in every district, to enforce these righteous edicts.

So perfectly was his will obeyed, that very soon the anarchy which had desolated the isles and wellnigh destroyed the people was entirely checked, and so complete a change effected, that the weakest and most helpless of his subjects could live in peace and security. In short, during the latter years of his reign, Hawaii began to enjoy something of a golden age. In order to curb the power of the conquered chiefs, and prevent them from hatching conspiracies against him, he retained them about his court, requiring them to accompany him wherever he went, nominally as his counsellors, but really to keep them away from their hereditary domains, where they might easily have stirred up discontent.

He made wise regulations concerning commerce, as also for the fisheries and modes of agriculture, and set his subjects an example by following all three pursuits himself, and excelling in each. He encouraged all useful handicrafts by bestowing rewards on the most skilful; and, in short, proved himself as wise and resolute in fostering all arts of peace, as he had ever been valiant and successful in war.

Not that he allowed his warriors to forget their cunning. All his subjects were required to keep their weapons in perfect order, so as to be ready for war at the shortest notice. Not content with this, he kept a standing army of regularly drilled soldiers, and enforced such severe discipline that death was the penalty for any breach of duty. He established armouries and magazines, erected forts and mounted batteries of heavy guns. He had six mortars, forty swivels, and abundant ammunition.

His fleet of foreign-built vessels, consisting of twenty schooners of from ten to fifty tons each, some of which carried guns, were well manned, and commanded by Europeans. He had also an

American ship, mounting twenty guns, and a vast number of war-canoes. So he was able to pass from isle to isle, and rule the whole archipelago more perfectly than his ancestors had ruled their one district on the great isle.

In old days the Hawaiians seem to have been always ready for fighting, and to have set about it in a most deliberate way. As a matter of course, every man was regularly drilled in the use of spear, javelin, sling and stone, and all other means of offence and defence. In time of war, all were required to follow their chief to the field; and any man who showed symptoms of cowardice, had his ears slit, and was led into the camp with a rope round his body—a measure which greatly assisted the nervous in overcoming their fears!

Some of their war customs were almost identical with those of the Fijians, as, for instance, the boastful shouts of defiance, and the advance of scouts, or of a single warrior, deridingly carrying only a fan, as if to brush away harmless flies, and challenging the foe to attack him singly. Perhaps, in reply, a dozen spears would be cast at him at once; and these he avoided by nimbly twisting or jumping aside, or stooping. Sometimes he caught them in his hands and hurled them back at his assailants. Truly, civilised warfare leaves us no such picturesque incidents as these.

The Hawaiians carried no banners; but the idols, borne by the priests, acted as rallying-points, and inspired the combatants with vigour. As flags of truce, they sent young banana-trees, whose broad and long silky green leaves waved as they moved. Then the chiefs and priests of both tribes met, to decide on terms of peace. This done, they sacrificed a pig, and poured its blood on the ground, as a symbol of the fate that awaited the truce-breaker. A wreath of the fragrant *mailé* was woven by the leaders of both sides, and deposited as their joint-offering in one of the temples. Heralds were then sent round to proclaim peace.

This happy result generally occurred when the opponents were well matched, in which case each acknowledged themselves to be *luka lua*,—*i.e.*, beaten. But if either party was victorious, then the vanquished were treated as slaves, and made to cultivate their own land for the conquerors: some were sacrificed on the altars of the blood-thirsty god of war, and their wives and children became the property of the victors.

Kamehameha's last great warlike demonstration was when he resolved on the conquest of Kauai (the northernmost isle), and assembled an army of seven thousand warriors and fifty whites, mostly armed with muskets. But ere he could embark on this expedition, a strange and unaccountable epidemic broke out, and swept over the isles, proving fatal to a great multitude of the people, and to many of the king's chief counsellors. So great was the mortality, that the living were not able to bury the dead. It is supposed to have been a form of Asiatic cholera.

One might naturally suppose that the king of Kauai would have considered this plague a special interposition of the gods on his behalf (as the action of Pélé had previously been for Kamehameha); but so far from this being the case, he seems to have held his adversary in so great respect, that he voluntarily ceded to him the supreme power, agreeing to hold his islands of Kauai and Niihau in fief from Kamehameha, in return for his protection—a peaceful solution of the difficulty, which seems to have given satisfaction to all parties.

The warrior-king fully understood the advantages of keeping up great external state: all the old customs and ceremonies observed by the ancient Hawaiian kings were rigidly enforced. Whenever he himself passed by, every creature present must crouch, and strip to the waist (this was the mark of deepest reverence to be observed on approaching a temple). The same act of homage was required by any person approaching his house, and also while the king's food and drink were being carried to him. His drinking-water was brought from springs far inland, specially reserved for his use; and all the country people were compelled to crouch and strip, retaining only the *malo*, or narrow girdle, when they heard the warning cry of the carriers bearing this precious burden.

But while keeping up these barbarous ceremonies, and adhering to native customs in regard to food and dwelling, he provided European houses for his foreign guests, and tables furnished with the crockery and knives and forks of civilisation. He had in his service a considerable number of foreign artisans, and even some physicians. Every encouragement was given to such white men as wished to settle on the isles; and by A.D. 1810, Oahu alone numbered sixty foreign residents. Amongst these were a certain proportion of steady industrious men, but unfortunately the majority appear to have been worthless vagabonds, deserters from whaling and other ships. Even the idle and dissolute, however, were held in restraint by the influence and authority of this master-mind.

Ever on the watch to acquire knowledge of every sort, nothing escaped his notice, and he encouraged his subjects to acquire all possible arts, so that very soon a considerable number of the natives became expert as carpenters, blacksmiths, coopers, and even tailors!

Much of the king's wealth was derived from the

trade in sandal-wood and in pearls. The former was so abundant that in one year it brought in a sum of 400,000 dollars. The chiefs very naturally looked upon it as an inexhaustible mine of wealth, and sorely were the people oppressed by the compulsory labour required of them to procure it.

If a chief wished to possess a vessel, he agreed with her owner to supply in exchange an amount of sandal-wood equal to the bulk of the craft. A pit was dug of her exact length, breadth, and depth, and this was filled with the precious wood, which was cut in the most wasteful and ruthless manner. As usual, the good sense of the king perceived how quickly such wholesale destruction would exhaust the forests, and he enacted laws for the preservation of the young timber—which, however, were so effectually evaded in later years, that here, as in the Polynesian isles, the sandal-wood tree is wellnigh extinct.

One of Kamehameha's bold enterprises was to purchase and fit up a vessel, officered by white men, which should run direct to Canton with a cargo of sandal-wood. Knowing of the large profits made by merchants in this trade, he hoped to realise a considerable sum; but, by the dishonesty of the ship's officers, the vessel returned with 3000 dollars of debt in lieu of profit. The ship's accounts were made out so as to show that the money had all been expended on exorbitant port charges, pilotage, anchorage, and custom-house dues. Ever ready to learn, even in so hard a school, the wise king at once perceived that he also might raise a revenue from these sources, as the number of foreign ships touching at Hawaii was rapidly increasing. Thenceforward regular rates for harbour dues were imposed.

While so very civilised a system of collecting revenue was established at the ports, the tax-gatherers of the interior had a strangely simple method of keeping their accounts. Having no knowledge of writing, they devised a most ingenious sort of ledger. It consisted of several hundred fathoms of cord, on which the different districts were represented by loops, tufts, and knots, of various sizes, shapes, and colours. Thus the different taxable articles, and their rates, were marked, and a record was kept of the resources of various provinces, and the amount of taxes rendered by each village. It certainly sounds a most perplexing form of *memoria technica*, but apparently its results were satisfactory.

Among the most valued of Kamehameha's new acquisitions were his horses. The first ever seen in the isles was brought from Boston in 1803. Ere long, others were imported from California, and the king soon became an accomplished rider,

—an example which his subjects have followed to the present day, when men and women scamper wildly all over the country, on the weediest of animals.

Rumours now reached Hawaii of the great changes wrought in Tahiti by the adoption of Christianity, and Kamehameha remembered the words of his friend Vancouver, and began to desire instruction from the foreign settlers concerning their religion. It is a painful commentary on the class of men who acted as the pioneers of civilisation, that he found none capable of teaching him the simplest outline of the Christian faith. "He no tell him nothing," was the comprehensive account given by a Hawaiian of this vain cry for light from the dark king to the white trader.

So this grand savage died as he had lived, worshipping the gods of his ancestors. In his last illness, when he became too weak even to turn on his mat, he called his son Liho Liho, and bade him go to the temple to make supplication on his behalf, adding that he himself would offer his prayers where he lay. So he prayed to his feather-god, Kukailimoku. Afterwards, a chief who had a bird-god called Pua, suggested that perhaps it might heal the king of his sickness; so it was brought, that its power might be tested, but it availed nothing, and on the 8th May 1819 (just forty years after Captain Cook's discovery of the isles), the master-mind—which had welded all these conflicting tribes into one united people—passed away, at the age of sixty-six.

To the last he maintained the oppressive and rigorous laws of the *tabu*, and only a few months before he died, three men were put to death for the most trivial infringements of arbitrary prohibitions. One was sacrificed for putting on a waist-cloth belonging to a chief, another for eating forbidden food, a third for leaving a house which had been placed under *tabu*, and entering another. A woman was likewise put to death for entering her husband's eating-house, though she was under the influence of drink when she ventured on this indiscretion.

The whole system of *tabu* was one long oppression. It affected all classes, though the priests and high chiefs took care that their share of the burden was a light one. But the common people were weighed down, from their birth to their graves, by the most senseless and cruel enactments. They were in constant danger of infringing some rigid rule of etiquette, for which the penalty was death. To bathe in a pool reserved for the chief; to touch his food, his clothing, his house; to walk in his shadow; to appear upright in his presence, or to approach him without baring the shoulders,—were offences punishable by death.

But the most trying *tabus* were those relating to the gods, which were proclaimed according to the caprice of the priests. Particular seasons were made *tabu*, during which, for weeks, or even months, the people must abstain from sports, or fishing, or house-building, or from certain foods. During these seasons, a man and woman who exchanged words, or even accidentally touched one another, were liable to be sacrificed; and the victims of the *tabu* had no easy death. Those who were simply strangled, stoned, or clubbed, were fortunate. Often the priests awarded lingering deaths of torture, lasting for several days. Eyes were scooped out, limbs broken, or the victims were burnt in a slow fire.

The institution of *tabu* was common to every group in Polynesia. The Hawaiian term was *kapu*. Its primary meaning was sanctity: hence the high chiefs, who held special privileges, as being descended from the gods, were called *alii kapu*, or sacred chiefs; the temples were *wahi kapu*, sacred places; and the things offered in sacrifice were especially *kapu*. The choicest hunting-grounds, the best fishing-coasts, the most fruitful lands, were made *kapu*, and reserved for the use of the sacred classes (a commoner venturing to trespass on these, would receive harder measure than even an unlucky tourist in a Scotch deer-forest, or a poacher on a favourite salmon-run!)

The priests periodically proclaimed that the gods required a season of *tabu*. Heralds were sent round to announce the edict, which none dared to disobey. If only a common *tabu* were required, it sufficed that the men should abstain from their ordinary avocations, and attend the morning and evening sacrifice at the temple. But when a season of strict *tabu* was ordered, then silence and gloom pervaded the land. Not a fire or a light was to be seen, not a canoe might be launched, — even bathing was prohibited; no one was allowed to leave his own house, save those who were required to officiate at the temples. No noise must be heard; even the mouths of dogs were tied up, lest they should bark; and the fowls were swathed in cloth, and put under calabashes, lest they should venture to cackle! During such a *tabu*, the chiefs and priests were interdicted from handling their own food, which was put into their mouths by their attendants. Any breach of these stringent regulations was supposed to displease the gods, and annul the benefits expected from the *tabu*.

But it was on women that the institution of *tabu* rested most oppressively, throughout their whole lives. It was death for a woman to approach a temple, to enter the eating-house of any man, even her husband. Never might she taste the food which had been cooked for a man, even when his meal was finished: hers might not even be cooked at the same fire. All the daintiest meats were reserved exclusively for the male animals,—I cannot call them lords of the creation; for all rank descended only from the female side, and the right of blood gave a woman power to rule all men of lower birth than herself.

But the highest chiefess—who thus held the power of life and death over her inferiors, and who had the right of selecting, and repudiating, any number of husbands at her own caprice—was as entirely subject to the iron law of *tabu* as the meanest of her attendants. The savoury meats on which her kinsmen feasted, might never pass her lips. Turtle, pork, and shark might be captured by her people, and certain excellent varieties of cocoa-nut and banana grown on her lands, for the use of her male relations, but she might never taste them. From its earliest infancy, a female child was taught to avoid the food that had touched its father's dish, as if it were poison.

For generation after generation, the people had been held enthralled by this system, which, in fact, became more and more oppressive as years rolled on. But with the arrival of foreigners came the dawn of deliverance. They were seen to infringe every *tabu* with impunity; and when at length some daring spirits were tempted secretly to follow their example, they found that so long as they escaped detection by the priests, the gods took no heed of their presumptuous actions. White men persuaded native women to eat with them, and even to taste the forbidden meats. Some were discovered, and fearfully beaten; but others enjoyed their feast so much as to risk a repetition of the offence. Finally, some of the chiefs began to think that the foreigners, who apparently acknowledged no religious obligation whatever, might be right, and that the priests were deceivers, the oracles lying words, and the service of the idols senseless folly.

As long as Kamehameha lived, none dared openly to infringe the laws which he upheld; but at his death, the flood-gates of scepticism were thrown open. The highest women of his family were the most advanced thinkers in the isles, and his son Liho Liho Iolani was thoroughly imbued with the infidelity of the white men, who were his chosen friends. He seems to have been a kindly and popular young fellow, though grievously dissolute, and much addicted to liquor.

The priests were allowed full sway till after the burial of the great king. They announced that the gods required the immediate sacrifice of a human victim, and that, should this offering be delayed till the morrow, forty men must die. How this matter was settled is not recorded; but three hundred dogs were sacrificed, and the people mourned after the usual manner, behaving like beasts and madmen.

When this indescribably revolting saturnalia was over, Liho Liho was robed in the royal mantle of feathers, and proclaimed king, under the title of Kamehameha II. His mother, the great chiefess Keopulani, urged him at once to break through the laws of *tabu*, and she set him the example by eating with her younger son; and Kaahumanu, the great king's favourite wife, who by his will was to retain a large share of power, gave the same counsel.

But Liho Liho still wavered, and for a while seems to have determined to support the priests. He even consecrated a new *heiau* to his especial god, and joined in the revelry and drunkenness of certain heathen festivals. Kaahumanu, however, continued firm in her determination to overthrow the *tabus*, which formed the key-stone of the whole system of idolatry, and sent word to the king that, on a given day, she intended openly to renounce his god, and to break through the *tabus*. Liho Liho, who had heard much about the part taken by King Pomare and the Tahitian chiefs in overthrowing idolatry in the Society Isles, and the benefits which had already resulted from the change, bethought him that it might be well to curtail the power of the priests, and to diminish the expenditure of labour and property in the service of the temples.

Finding that several of the high chiefs were willing to support him, he invited them all to a great feast. According to custom, the women assembled in a place apart. So soon as the food was prepared, and the pigs, fowls, turtles, and certain *tabued* fish were cut up, the king bade his attendants carry these forbidden dainties to his wives and the other women, with whom he then sat down to eat.

Shouts of amazement from the multitude greeted this breach of the *tabu*; but the king's example was followed by several chiefs, who thus deliberately violated the oppressive system which, in a thousand details, had weighed on each man, woman, and child from the hour of their birth.

Of course the majority of the priests threatened terrible consequences from the wrath of the gods; but Heva-heva, the high priest of the war-god, declared that no evil would ensue, even if the worship of the gods were altogether discontinued. Thereupon he resigned his office, and the king announced that both idols and priests should be utterly abolished.

Several of the priests supported the action of Heva-heva, and seem actually to have taken part in the destruction of idols and demolition of *heiaus* which followed. The sacred relics, which had for ages been objects of devout worship, were committed to the flames, and the rejoicing people began to realise that their days of thraldom were ended.

But it was not to be supposed that such an upheaval could occur without opposition, or that the great mass of the priests would let the iconoclasts run riot through all sacred places without opposition.

By the will of Kamehameha, his nephew Kekuao-kalani had been appointed to share with Liho Liho in the general charge of the temples and the support of the national worship. To him the priestly party now looked as to their rightful champion. Assuring him of victory, and of the certainty of obtaining for himself the sovereignty of the isles, they raised a strong force, and flew to arms in the name of the insulted gods.

The followers of the king were equally prompt in preparing for battle, and the two factions met on the sea-shore of Isle Hawaii, and fought to the death. The action continued ten hours, when the conservative-ecclesiastical party were effectually routed. Most of the leaders perished, faithful to their cause.

As the day wore on, Kekuao-kalani, though sorely wounded, and weak from loss of blood, made a last stand to rally his flying forces; but receiving a ball in the breast, he covered his face with his feather cloak, and expired.

His faithful wife Manona had never left his side throughout that hardly-contested day, but fought with dauntless courage. A few moments after her husband fell, a ball struck her on the temple, and she fell dead upon the corpse of her lord. The battle-field is still strewn with many cairns, one of which, larger than the rest, marks the spot where the brave young chief and his noble wife were slain; while, nearer the sea, an oblong pile of stones was raised over the grave in which they were laid, and a thick carpet of the lilac marine convolvulus quickly overspread the tomb.

It seems to have been no uncommon thing for women to accompany their husbands into the thick of battle, bearing in one hand a calabash of water or of *poi*, wherewith to recruit their lords when exhausted, and in the other hand a spear for their own defence. Even if they did not actually take part in the fight, women generally accompanied the warriors, to nurse them should they be wounded.

There was one feature of old Hawaiian warfare which is specially interesting on account of its similarity to ancient Hebrew custom,—namely, that of having cities of refuge—*puhonuas*, as they were called—which afforded an inviolable sanctuary to all who were in any danger, either when fleeing from victorious foes or from justice. There were two such places on Hawaii. One was at Honaù-naù; the other at Waipio, in the district of Kohala.

The former was a large enclosure, with several wide entrances facing in every direction; so that the fugitives, whether coming from north, south, east, or west, might make straight running for their haven. At a short distance beyond each gate was planted a tall spear, from which fluttered a white flag.

Thus far might the pursuer follow his foe, but not one step farther. Should he do so, he would himself be guilty of desecrating the *pahu tabu*— *i.e.*, the sacred enclosure—and the priests of Keave would show no mercy to such criminals, who would assuredly be put to death; though the man who had broken any other *tabu*, or was a thief, a manslayer, or even a murderer, was safe the moment he crossed the threshold.

The first act of the fugitive was to give thanks in presence of the image of Keave, and he was then allowed to rest in one of the houses built specially for refugees, within the sanctuary; and here he must remain for a few days, after which he might return to his home.

The *puhonua* at Honaù-naù was on a very large scale—so large as to afford refuge to all the women, children, and weakly folk of the neighbourhood, in time of war. It was about 700 feet long by 400 wide, and was surrounded by walls 12 feet high and 15 in thickness. Within it were built three large *heiaus*, or sacred platforms. One of these was 126 feet by 65, and 10 feet high. Several masses of lava-rock, weighing two or three tons apiece, were built into the solid wall, at some height from the ground, exciting a feeling of marvel as to how such cyclopean work had been performed, by savages ignorant of all mechanical appliances. It was said to have been built for Keave, who reigned in Hawaii in the seventeenth century.

The other *puhonua* was at Pakarana, in the Waipio district; and though not so large as that at Honaù-naù, it was nevertheless a large enclosure, and a place of great antiquity. Within it was a small mausoleum overshadowed by a fine old screw-pine. This was the *Ke Hale o Riroa*,[1] and contained the bones of Riroa, who reigned in Hawaii about eighteen generations back. His rudely carved stone image stood at one corner of the sanctuary, and to it all comers made offerings of hogs; and the successive kings, if unable to visit it in person, sent their gifts by deputy.

The battle of which we have been speaking was

[1] The House of Riroa.

fought within a short distance of the principal *puhonua*. The victory there gained by Liho Liho completed the overthrow of idol-worship, which was already tottering to its fall. For many years a moral dry-rot had been at work, and there remained only a mouldering outward form, which had ceased to retain any hold on the hearts of the people, and was only supported through superstitious fear.

These very remarkable events occurred in November 1819.

CHAPTER XVII.

HAWAIIAN MORALS — DRESS — HAIR-DRESSING — COMMENCEMENT OF THE MISSION—A BLIND DANCER—KING AND QUEEN VISIT ENGLAND AND DIE — PERNICIOUS INFLUENCE OF CERTAIN FOREIGNERS.

You perceive that the abolition of idolatry in Hawaii was an entirely spontaneous action, — an almost accidental consequence of the overthrow of the *tabu* system. The only foreign influence traceable in the matter was that of men who, hating all law, felt that the restraints of the *tabu* sometimes indirectly affected themselves, and who, in any case, were ready to promote any measure which tended to more unbridled licence.

To this the Hawaiians needed small encouragement; so the practical result of a measure which had been carried out by the king when in a condition of semi-intoxication, and which left his country without any form of religion, or any definite law, was to produce a state of anarchy, of which "the mean whites" were not slow to take advantage. And, as a natural consequence, immorality in all its most flagrant forms is said to have reached a climax hitherto unknown, even in Hawaii. Yet so unspeakable had been the debasement of the people in past years, that there scarcely could have been room for much deterioration. The young naval officer who filled up his official report on some such race as this with "Manners—None; Customs—Beastly," would certainly have been justified, had his subject been Hawaii.

Every element that can be said to constitute social degradation, flourished unchecked. Aged and infirm persons were frequently buried alive, or cast from a precipice, by their own children, who could not be troubled to take care of them. Still more frequently they were turned out of the houses their own hands had reared, and left to die by the roadside, unpitied and untended — their corpses being devoured by wild dogs. The blind or deformed were only suffered to live as a butt for cruel jesters. Idiots and lunatics, though occasionally treated with reverence as an incarnation of some god, were frequently stoned to death.

Compassion and sympathy seem to have been unknown virtues. If a man were in any difficulty, if his house took fire, or he was in any way hurt, or if his chief frowned on him, it was the signal for his neighbours to persecute him, and despoil him of his goods.

Cannibalism (which the native historians affirm to have been the common practice of their ancestors,[1] when, after a battle, they roasted the slain) had fallen into disrepute before the days of Captain Cook, and was then confined to certain robber chieftains, who infested the mountains and forests, thence making raids on their more peaceable neighbours, and carrying them off, to furnish loathsome feasts. The warriors who did battle with these dreaded ghouls, became heroes of Hawaiian chivalry, and their praises were celebrated in songs and dances.

At the same time, there must have been another way of looking upon this revolting practice; for, in the native records of the death of the great king, it is related that the high chiefs held counsel, how they could best show their reverent devotion to the dead, and the first spokesman said, "This is my thought—*we will eat him raw!*" To which the chief widow replied — not disapproving the suggestion, but merely doubtful—"Perhaps his body is not at our disposal: that rests with his succes-

---

[1] History of the Hawaiian Islands. By J. J. Jarves. P. 91. Published Boston, 1843.

sor." And so the body was taken to the consecrated house for the performance of the proper rites by the priest and the king. And when the sacred hog was baked, the priest offered it to the dead body, *and it became a god*, the king at the same time repeating the customary prayers.

Certainly, however, this ingredient of horror had almost, if not entirely, ceased to exist, before white men had much intercourse with these isles, but crime in other forms abounded. It is a somewhat significant point of comparison between the Fijians and the Hawaiians, that the former, while they indulged in cannibalism to an unparalleled extent, were so particular with regard to their women, that they occupied separate houses, and it was a punishable offence for a man even to touch a woman's sleeping-mat. Every girl was betrothed in early youth, and her future husband shared with her parents the responsibility of her careful guardianship, strangling being the penalty that awaited both culprits in case of transgression.

But in Hawaii no such feeling existed. Men and women, lads and lasses, all herded together promiscuously, one large sheet of *tappa* acting as the household blanket.

The houses of the great chiefs were sometimes carpeted with beautifully variegated mats, perhaps twenty yards in length by four in width; but the houses of the people were, for the most part, filthy hovels, consisting merely of a thatched roof, without any walls to raise it from the ground. The floor was merely strewn with dried grass, and swarmed with vermin.

Infanticide seems to have prevailed throughout the Hawaiian isles to an extent even more awful than in the Society group, and in an aggravated form. Although the Tahitians rarely allowed more than two of the largest family to be reared, yet if from any cause a child was allowed to survive its birth even a few hours, its parents rarely could bring themselves to murder it.

But the Hawaiians appear to have been far more inhuman, for multitudes of children were put to death when they were several months old. If they chanced to be unusually fretful, or their parents found them particularly inconvenient, they were unscrupulously suffocated. A hole was dug in the earthen floor of the house, and the wailing baby was therein deposited, a bit of cloth thrust into its mouth to still its cries, the earth and mats replaced, and quiet being thus restored, domestic life continued peaceful as before.

The Tahitians at least buried their dead out of their sight, seeking some retired corner in the bush wherein to lay the unwelcomed child-angels. In Hawaii, sheer idle selfishness seems to have been the cause of a crime which led to the destruction *of two-thirds of the population.* The high chiefs, who had both property and attendants, spared such children as were born to them, though these were few,—partly, no doubt, in consequence of their atrocious customs of intermarriage — children of the same parents being considered suitable mates. In fact, among members of the blood-royal the marriage of brothers and sisters was supposed to be the only safeguard for the purity of the race. Failing these, uncles married their nieces, or nephews their aunts: nor was there any objection to a father and son having one wife in common.

But apart from connections so repulsive as these, the morals of the Hawaiians could be best summed up as " none." Domestic life was altogether promiscuous—husbands and wives being interchangeable at pleasure. As regarded children, it was not merely a wise child who knew its own father, but some discrimination was required to know its mother; for most women gave away their expected little one before its birth, to any one who could be bothered with so troublesome a gift. If no one offered to adopt the poor little stranger, then the inhuman mother buried it alive.

Multitudes of women told the early missionaries that they had with their own hands buried seven or eight of their children. And sometimes a pitying neighbour arrived in time to dig up the newly buried baby, and rear it herself, when, of course, it grew up with slight knowledge of its mother, who had probably devoted all her petting (I cannot use the word affection) to some favourite piggy or puppy, which she suckled in preference to her child, and which grew up to be a somewhat unlovable inmate.

One of the queens who had thus reared a fine young hog, and who subsequently became a very devout Christian, found its affection rather inconvenient, when, having grown to a great size, and armed with large tusks, it insisted on taking its place in chapel, as beseemed a knowing and intelligent hog.

"A lady loved a swine! 'Humph!' quoth he.
'Piggy,' said she, 'wilt thou be mine?' 'Humph!' quoth he."

Our familiar household rhyme would have been eminently descriptive of a Hawaiian lady and her dainty pet. As a matter of course, the pigs, dogs, and ducks of the establishment were recognised as favoured members of the family, eating out of the same bowl as the children—a custom not altogether unknown in some corners of the British Isles in this nineteenth century!

Although the Hawaiians cannot be said to have recognised any manner of sanctity in their marriage ties, yet, in the case of some of the high chiefs, the *tabu* seems to have secured something approaching to it, as culprits were occasionally beheaded—a mild and merciful punishment compared with that awarded to the man found guilty of robbery from a great chief. On some of the isles the thief was bound hand and foot, placed on a rotten old canoe, towed out to sea, and there turned adrift—a Mazeppa at the mercy of the sea-horses, utterly helpless, only craving that the canoe might speedily sink, and so save him from the anguish of a lingering death from thirst and starvation.

In the presence of such a civilised community as the Hawaiians of to-day, and of ladies whose fashionably made silks and satins are supplied by expensive American milliners, it is scarcely credible that only sixty years ago a sail in the offing was the signal for all these nut-brown maids and matrons, from the highest chiefess to her lowliest vassal, to swim out to sea to welcome the new-comers.

"But though on pleasure they were bent,
They all had frugal minds,"

and were nowise disposed to wet the scanty drapery of *tappa* which had cost them so much labour to prepare. So this was carefully left at home; and these economical daughters of Eve plunged into the surf with no bathing-dress save their long raven tresses, and thus they boarded the vessels, and there established themselves, drying their long hair in the sun like a troop of mermaidens.

So utterly unconscious were these Hawaiians of any conventional ideas of impropriety in the matter of undress, that (like worthy Japanese couples taking their air-bath after a hot-bath) these invariably left their clothes at home if they were likely to get wet, and had no hesitation in calling on their friends in this light marching order.

When the first missionaries came to the isles, the king came on board to dine with them; and the ladies of the mission, fresh from New England, were rather surprised at the Royal costume, which consisted of a narrow waist-girdle, a green silk scarf thrown over the shoulders, a necklace of large beads, and a crown of scarlet feathers. But when, a few days later, they were established in a house on shore, they were much more startled by repeated visits from the king, accompanied by his five wives, all alike guiltless of any manner of garment. On their suggesting that this was not altogether in accordance with civilised ideas, the king made a point of complying with the hint, so came next day fully attired in a pair of silk stockings and a cocked-hat!

That dreadful hat was quickly followed by all the other hideous garments of the foreigners; and within three years, the king and all his chiefs were attired in shirts, vests, pants, coats, stockings, shoes, gloves, and hats! Oh poor chiefs!—how they must have longed for the cool airy undress of old days! Imagine these children of the tropics finding their throats encased in the high shirt-collars and stiff stocks of the Georges! Such is the costume in which King Liho Liho is handed down to posterity.

A somewhat picturesque era intervened ere the court was wholly given over to the rigid regulation patterns, as ruled by inexorable tailors. Thus, at a festival celebrating the death of Kamehameha I., which was kept up for several days (after a great company of natives, all clothed in white, had laid their annual taxes at the feet of King Liho Liho), there was a procession in honour of his five queens, in which things new and old blended in the oddest manner.

First, Queen Kamamalu was borne aloft in state, seated in a whale-boat, placed on a platform of wicker-work thirty feet long by twelve wide. The boat and the framework were covered with foreign broad-cloth and handsome native *tappa*. The queen was robed in scarlet silk, and wore a feather crown. A chief stood beside her wearing a feather helmet, and supporting an immense Chinese umbrella, highly gilt, and decorated with scarlet tassels and fringes. Two of the highest chiefs stood behind her on the platform, wearing waist-cloths of scarlet silk, and helmets of yellow feathers that shone in the sun. Each carried a *kahili* (the bottle-brush emblem of royalty), with its plume of scarlet feathers, about twelve feet in height, mounted on a handle about twenty feet high, adorned with alternate rings of tortoise-shell and ivory.

The whole of this erection was carried along on the shoulders of seventy men, marching in solid phalanx. The *show*-men on the outer ranks were resplendent in gleaming cloaks and helmets of glossy feathers—scarlet and yellow.

The king's brother and sister were carried along in similar style, seated in double canoes, placed on a platform covered with *tappa*, and with a canopy of yellow cloth. Behind them stood two very high chiefs, bearing dishes of baked dog, raw fish, and a calabash of *poi*, to note their own lowliness in relation to the Royal children. The latter wore the simple *malo* and *pau*—the male and female native dress—but made of scarlet silk.

The two queens-dowager were gorgeously apparelled. One of these portly dames was swathed in seventy yards of cashmere, half orange and half scarlet, forming such a bale of stuff that her arms were supported horizontally, while the surplus formed a train carried by her attendants.

One of the queens indulged in a little extravaganza. When a child, she had narrowly escaped being burnt to death—hence she had ever since borne the name of Pauahi (*ahi*, fire). On the present occasion, she thought fit to commemorate the event; so when, after the procession, she alighted from her couch, she set it on fire, with all its decorations, and further, threw in the whole of her clothing, except a small handkerchief—an example followed by all her retinue; so that much good foreign and native cloth was sacrificed for this little display!

Meanwhile several hundred singers and dancers were making merry, and their wild choruses, rude music, and deafening drums mingled with the acclamations of thousands of spectators, all gaily decorated with feather necklaces or wreaths of flowers.

The revels were kept up for a week—a great house of feasting, like a fairy bower, having been prepared for the occasion. The king and his suite added to the excitement, if not to the safety, of the multitude, by riding barebacked horses in the most reckless manner.

A considerable number of these revellers atoned for the scantiness of their raiment by their elaborate permanent decoration. The tattooers of Hawaii appear to have aimed at subjects as difficult as those we still find in Japan.[1] Ellis described one

[1] In 'A Lady's Cruise in a French Man-of-War,' vol. ii., p. 165, I

man as having no less than six goats thus indelibly imprinted on his face—namely, two goats rampant on the forehead, one on each side of the nose, and one at each corner of the mouth. Round his eyes were tattooed Vandyck semicircles. A long bunch of jet-black curling hair hung down behind each ear, and a heavy curl rested on his forehead, the rest of the head being close-cropped, while the upper part of the beard was braided, then tied in a knot, and the ends spread out in curls. He was lightly draped, and a large palm-leaf fan gave the finishing touch to this dandy of the isles.

In nothing is the individuality of races more strikingly exemplified than in the fashions of hairdressing, and in no respect does the levelling effect of so-called civilisation more quickly declare itself. Even the skilful barbers of Japan find their occupation passing from them, as the rising generation abandon the *queue* and shaven crown of their

---

ventured to propound a theory that the isles of the Eastern Pacific had been peopled, not directly by colonists from the West, as is generally assumed, but by the descendants of those Malays who, having first travelled northward to Formosa and Japan, had thence been drifted by south-westerly currents to the Sandwich Isles and the southern group.

I have recently been informed that about the year 1850 a Japanese junk was driven out of its course by adverse weather, and then drifted all the way to the Sandwich Isles, several of the crew having survived the perilous voyage. This certainly tends to confirm the possibility of a circuitous migration.

ancestors and adopt the simple cropped head of the Anglo-Saxon.

Throughout the Pacific, each island differed from all its neighbours in the eccentric modes of hair-dressing adopted by its people. In Fiji, each chief had his special barber, whose sole work in life was to devise fearful and wonderful methods of torturing his master's hair.

Here, in Hawaii, the same custom prevailed. Some wore their hair tied into a single huge round bunch on the top of the head; so that, at a short distance, a man appeared to have two heads, one on the top of the other. Some preferred to wear it in five or six smaller bunches; others endeavoured to shape their heads after the same model as a crested helmet, by cutting all their hair close, with the exception of a ridge five inches wide extending from the forehead to the neck. The hair being thick and curly, stood up like a mane, and gave the wearer quite a martial appearance. This style of hair-dressing was a symbol of mourning for the dead, when it was necessary to cut some portion of the hair. Others again, not disdaining the use of false hair, wore large clusters of long ringlets flowing down their backs.

Now all heads are as much alike in form as in colour, being clipped on the simplest American model.

The mission history of Hawaii has been an era of very smooth sailing, as compared with that of most other groups in the Pacific. Strange to say, although British missionary efforts were directed to Tahiti, and other South Sea isles, so early as A.D. 1796, no attempt was made to establish any footing in the Sandwich Isles until the year 1820, when the American Board of Foreign Missions at Boston found themselves in a position to send out an efficient staff to try what could be done in this group. The idea had been suggested some years previously, when one morning the students at Yale College found a dark-skinned lad sitting on the door-step crying bitterly. He told them how his father and mother had been slain before his eyes; and when he fled, carrying his infant brother on his back, the child was killed with a spear, and he was taken prisoner. After a while he managed to get on board an American ship, and so landed at New Haven. Craving to be taught all the wisdom of white men, he found his way to the College, hoping by some means to gain access to it. But at the last his heart had failed him, and so, sad and lonely, he could not choose but weep.

Kind hearts were moved. The poor lad was taken as a pupil, and received the teaching he craved. After a while, Opukahaia became so deeply impressed with the reality of the Christian faith, that he confided to others his longing to go back to Hawaii and tell the good news to his countrymen. The idea thus started, gradually expanded, and white men determined that the young convert should not return alone on his perilous enterprise. Four other young Hawaiians were received at the College, and the idea of forming a special mission to the Sandwich Isles took definite form.

But Opukahaia was not destined himself to carry the Gospel to his dear isles. Ere his own studies were completed, he was called away from this lower school. But the great longing of his heart had awakened an echo in many others, and in the autumn of 1819 (at the very time when King Liho Liho was abolishing the *tabu* and destroying the idols) a mission band of seventeen persons was preparing to embark at Boston.

The party consisted of the Rev. Hiram Bingham, the Rev. Asa Thurston; Dr Holman, a physician; Daniel Chamberlain, a farmer; Samuel Whitney, mechanic and teacher; Samuel Ruggles, catechist and teacher; and Elisha Loomis, printer and teacher. All were accompanied by their wives, and the farmer had a family of five children. One of the Hawaiian lads (Kamaulii) was son to the king of Kauai.

Knowing what dangers had beset the pioneer missionaries in all the other groups, the people of

Boston were keenly interested in their undertaking, and crowds assembled to witness the ordination of Messrs Bingham and Thurston. Six hundred communicants met for the farewell service; and so far from the mission party receiving undue encouragement, they were reminded, in a farewell charge, that "probably not one of them would live to see the downfall of idolatry." And so, doubtless, they all thought.

On the 23d October 1819, they embarked on the brig Thaddeus. On the 31st March 1820, they sighted the snow-capped peaks of Mauna Kea, and, as they neared the land, the Hawaiian lads put off in a boat to meet a fishing-canoe. A few minutes later the boat was seen returning, and the lads shouted in wild excitement, "Oahu's idols are no more!" Returning on board, they related the wonderful news told them by the fishers,—that the great king was dead—that Liho Liho had abolished the *tabu*, and burnt the idols.

Well was it for the simple folk that these teachers of righteousness arrived amongst them at this critical time, for adverse influences were rife, in the form of a multitude of the very coarsest specimens of the white race, who annually found their way hither in the whaling ships, to which Honolulu proved a convenient station for refitting and provisioning. Consequently, in spring and autumn the island of Oahu was overrun with whalers, whose presence nowise tended to the moral weal of the people. It was nothing uncommon to see a fleet of from forty to sixty whaling ships anchored off the isle, bartering foreign goods for fresh meat and fruits; and the rowdyism of life ashore was by no means an improving example.

Such white men as had already settled on the isles, being mostly of this class, they naturally viewed the arrival of the mission party with small satisfaction, and strove by every means in their power to set the king and chiefs against them. First, they assured them that the strangers had come to take forcible possession of the land. "Then," said the chiefs, "they would not have brought their women." The white men then declared that the king of England, to whom Hawaii looked for protection, would be insulted if these Americans were allowed to land.

During a weary fortnight the travellers (craving to set foot on land after their five months' voyage in the little vessel) were confined to the ship. But at last the king decided to allow them to settle in the isles for one year, with the proviso that, should they prove unworthy, they were then to be banished. A native house was assigned to them; and no sooner had they landed, than the vessel hired to convey them thither, set sail, carrying off the three years' supplies provided by the Boston Mission, and leaving them with one barrel of salt beef, one of flour, and one of pork.

Here, then, they were left planted in Kailua Bay, on the great isle of Hawaii. The loss of stores was happily made up by the kindness of both chiefs and people. But of course these pioneers had to dispense with a multitude of things which *we* deem necessaries of life. Many years elapsed before milk could be obtained, even for the children; and it must have been rather trying at first for a whole party to have to live in a thatched hut, with only one room to act as sitting-room, feeding-room, bedroom, nursery, and study, all combined, to say nothing of the crowds of curious spectators, with wondering eyes, never weary of staring.

Mr Stewart gives us the dimensions of the house which was assigned to him and his family. It was 14 feet in length by 12 in breadth; its grass walls were only 3 feet high, and the ridge-pole supporting the heavy thatched roof was only 9 feet from the ground. Four openings cut through the thatch acted as door and windows; nevertheless, such close quarters can scarcely have been other than stifling in the tropics.

Strange to say, the foremost in giving cordial welcome to "his brother priests," as he called them, was Hewa-hewa, late high priest of the god of war, a very remarkable man. It was he who counselled the king to destroy the idols, telling him that wooden images, carved by their own hands, could never make the *kalo* to grow, nor send rain, nor bestow life and health; and, he added, " my thought has always been, 'there is only one Great God dwelling in the heavens.'" So now, when the servants of the One God arrived, he threw his whole weight on their side, and helped them by every means in his power.

The mission band was divided into three parties, to commence work at different points on the three principal islands; but the king and the chiefs claimed as their prerogative that they must be taught to read and write before that privilege was extended to the people. So heartily did the king enter into this new pursuit, that within four months he could read English intelligibly, and the chiefs were not far behind him in progress. Then schools for the people were opened, and a hundred scholars applied themselves to the double task of mastering the alphabet and the English language.

Meanwhile the missionaries were devoting themselves to the study of Hawaiian, and of reducing the language to writing; but two years elapsed ere their work was sufficiently advanced to enable them to begin printing on a small scale.

Unfortunately, the support given by the king was

of a very unstable nature. Kindly, but very wayward and dissipated, he was greatly influenced by the worthless vagabonds—French and English—by whom he was surrounded, and who strove by every means to counteract all good instruction. So the king vacillated between these opposite factions, one day promising a speedy reformation, the next joining his boon companions in bouts of bestial drunkenness and dissipation. His taste for gambling was assiduously encouraged by men who profited largely by his losses,—to supply which, the people were heavily taxed. Vast quantities of sandal-wood were cut in the most reckless manner, involving severe labour and oppression of the people, who were forced to work by tyrannical task-masters: many died from over-exertion and exposure, and the humane laws instituted by the great king Kamehameha I. were altogether set aside.

But some of the chiefs and chief women gave more earnest heed to the teaching of the newcomers, and foremost among the latter was Keopuolani, the king's mother, who by birth was the highest chiefess of Hawaii. On the death of her husband, the great Kamehameha, she married Hoapili, the governor of Maui, who fully shared his wife's anxiety to learn the new religion.

The name of Keopuolani holds an honoured place in Hawaiian story, as that of the first native who was deemed worthy to receive Christian baptism.

For two years the work of the missionaries was constantly impeded by the machinations of white men, who strove to persuade the king to send them away, on the pretext that the presence of American teachers would surely prove offensive to England.

Happily, however, in the spring of 1822, Messrs Tyerman and Bennet, deputed by the London Mission to visit all missionary stations in the Pacific, arrived at Oahu, accompanied by the Rev. William Ellis, who had for some time been working at Tahiti. The cordial meeting of these brother workers quickly proved to the natives how false were the statements which had been made to them; and at the joint request of the American Mission and the chiefs, Mr Ellis agreed to return to Tahiti, and to bring his wife and family to Hawaii for a year.

In 1823, a second party arrived from Boston, consisting of three ministers, two licensed preachers, and a physician, with their families. The king showed his goodwill to the new-comers by remitting the exorbitant harbour dues, and otherwise making them welcome.

Thus the Mission was fairly established, and the great truths of Christianity were proclaimed to all who could be induced to listen. Mr Ellis has recorded that "the new revelations were received with much attention, with wonder, and often with delight. The greater part of the people seemed to regard the tidings of 'endless life by Jesus' as the most joyful news they had ever heard, breaking upon them, to use their own expression, like light in the morning."

Some of those who were present on these occasions declared that the news was indeed good news, and added, "Let us all attend to it: who is there that does not desire eternal life in the other world?"

Others said: "Our forefathers, from time immemorial, and we, ever since we can remember anything, have been seeking the *ora roa* (enduring life), or a state in which we should not die, but we have never found it yet; perhaps this is it of which you are telling us."

Amongst those to whom the good tidings came home with an intense reality, was a wretched blind dancer, by name Puaaiki. His blindness was partly due to the excessive use of the intoxicating *kava* (here called *awa*), and his life had been as disreputable as it well could be. He was chiefly noted for his skill in the performance of the *hula-hula*, a combination of objectionable songs and dances. For this reason, he was retained for the amusement of the queen and chiefs, and earned a scanty living by playing the buffoon in their presence.

As a court-follower,[1] he accompanied the king to Honolulu, where he fell ill. Neglected and miserable, he lay alone, and the deep darkness that had blinded his eyes lay heavy on his soul. In this hour of distress he was found by Honolii, one of the Hawaiian lads educated in America, who comforted him, and spoke of the Great Physician who had given sight to the blind.

These words were as a message of life to the poor blind buffoon. He induced a heathen lad to lead him day after day to the place where the Christian teachers spoke to the people, and eagerly he drank in every word that was spoken. Those who observed him, saw only a picture of extreme degradation and wretchedness — a frail object of diminutive stature, and bowed down by sickness, with long black beard, and a scanty strip of bark cloth as his only dress. But his sightless eyes seemed to save him from distraction, and enabled him to give undivided attention to all he heard. His wonderful memory seemed to grasp everything, and to retain it indelibly.

When next the chiefs sent for him to come and

[1] When a high chief travelled from isle to isle, the multitude of followers was something amazing. Thus, when the queen-dowager sailed for Kauai in 1822, to collect the annual tribute of sandal-wood, she was accompanied by a retinue of twelve hundred persons, all of whom were crowded into four small vessels. Of course the feeding of so great a multitude was a very serious additional tax on the island thus visited.

dance before them, he refused, saying that henceforth he must live as beseemed a servant of the living God. Some derided him; but the queen respected his courage, and herself gave ear to the words of the poor blind dancer, who now besought her to seek the way of salvation.

In what appears an excess of caution, the missionaries refused to receive him as a member of the Church till they had kept him for four years on probation. They showed the same extreme care in regard to all who wished to join them, lest any should afterwards bring discredit on their profession.

But though thus kept, as it were, in an outer sanctuary, the earnestness and eloquence of the blind convert were felt to be a living influence. If his bodily presence was weak, his speech was with power; and when, at prayer-meetings, he was called upon to speak, all who heard him were touched to the heart by the deep pathos, and tenderness, and unutterable humility, with which he poured forth his soul as to One very near him.

Strange to say, fourteen years more were allowed to elapse ere this very devoted servant of the Lord was permitted to work officially as a deacon, and two years more ere he was licensed to preach. He had long been recognised as the most eloquent speaker in the nation, while his extraordinary memory made him more thoroughly master of the Scriptures than most men endowed with sight.

But these early American missionaries were slow to make full use of native agencies, and it was not till 1843 (the beginning of his last year on earth) that Batimea (*i.e.*, Bartimeus, the name chosen by the blind man at his baptism) was ordained as an evangelist.

There was at that time a great awakening throughout the district where he was called to labour, and besides visiting ceaselessly from house to house, he had constantly to journey to and fro on foot, between two villages twenty miles apart; so the willing spirit succumbed to the weary flesh, and the good servant whose promotion on earth had been so slow, was called to serve in the very presence of the Master.

He was noted to the last for the touching humility which ever took the lowest place and shrank every word of praise. His marvellous power of language, and his familiarity with all customs, legends, and modes of thinking, in the old religion, as well as his practical knowledge of the new faith, gave him such power as no foreigner ever attained, and the very fact of his blindness lent a deeper pathos to his earnest pleadings with his unseen hearers.

Immediately after his own conversion, he accompanied Keopuolani, the good queen-dowager, to her home at Lahaina on Maui, where she devoted herself to the study of the English Bible, which she had learnt to read—a difficult matter, as you may believe, and one which proved her determination to learn all about the new faith.

In the autumn she was seized with fatal illness, and summoned the king (her son) and all the chiefs. Earnestly she pleaded with Liho Liho that he should give up his career of dissipation and drunkenness, and most especially she charged him that she should be buried as a Christian, and that none of the horrible excesses practised at the death of a high chief should be tolerated. Then she called for the missionaries, and prayed that she might receive Christian baptism ere she passed away.

The solemn rite was administered; and soon afterwards, the first Christian of Hawaii, and highest chiefess of the isles, was carried to the tomb by the five queens of Liho Liho, and another high chiefess; and though the people wept and wailed exceedingly, the command of the king was obeyed, and no heathen rites profaned the funeral of the good queen-mother.

The stones of a dilapidated old heathen altar formed a convenient quarry from which to build a wall around her grave, and all the chiefs assisted in this work with their own hands. Kaahumanu, the proud queen-dowager, and her new husband, both huge and unwieldy, as beseemed high chiefs, were among those who toiled along, bearing large stones, in token of love to the dead, while strong men walked lazily after them, carrying only the light feather *kahilis* as the badge of their authority.

For a little while after his mother's death, Liho Liho seemed really to have turned over a new leaf; but his bad companions were quite resolved that the good impressions thus produced should not last long. Finding that he steadily refused to join their riotous Sunday parties, they at last persuaded him to go on board a newly arrived vessel, to inspect some new goods. All his favourite accustomed drinks were temptingly offered to him, but he refused to touch them. At last cherry-brandy, which he had never seen, was produced, with the assurance that it could not intoxicate, and, weary of refusing, he yielded. Of course the insatiable longing was reawakened, and his entertainers plied him with glass after glass, till they had accomplished their end, and a drunken revel ensued, in which the whole ingenuity of the white men was devoted to teaching their victim every form of blasphemy which the most horrible profanity could devise.

In presence of such a Royal example, the edicts

against drunkenness proclaimed by Kaahumanu, the queen-dowager, could have had little weight.

As usual, the king was very penitent after this outbreak; and when, a little later, he decided on making a voyage to England, he desired that the Rev. William Ellis should bear him company, as interpreter and counsellor. This, however, was by no means the intention of his advisers. Consequently the captain of the vessel—L'Aigle—declared it was positively impossible for him to provide accommodation for the Ellis family, though a considerable sum was offered as their passage-money.

The motives which prompted this refusal were very evident, when, on reaching London, the king's treasure-chests, which had been sent on board containing 25,000 dollars, were forwarded to the Bank of England, where, on their being opened, only 10,000 dollars were found remaining!

Wretchedly weak as he was, Liho Liho was dearly loved by his people; and in after-years, Hawaiian mothers loved to tell how graciously he had kissed their little ones, ere he sailed on that long voyage to the distant British Isles, from which it was fated that he might not return in life.

Still better loved was his sister and queen, Kamcha-maru (which means, shade of Kamcha, in graceful allusion to her father, the great Kamehameha—the father also of Liho Liho!) Happily the impressions made on her mind by the words of the poor blind dancer had deepened and taken definite form. She was emphatically the friend of her people, always striving to do good in every possible way. She was one of the first to embrace Christianity, and used all her influence to induce her subjects to do likewise. She erected the first Christian school at Honolulu, where about forty pupils were taught to read and write, and she and her chief women took the keenest interest in their progress.

When the day came on which she was to embark for England, the grief of the Hawaiians knew no bounds. The king had already embarked on board L'Aigle, and a boat was waiting the coming of the queen. As she passed through the crowd on her way to the shore, those near her fell on their knees and kissed her feet, weeping bitterly, while the thousands who thronged the beach made loud wailings, in unfeigned sorrow.

When she reached the shore she paused, and in the manner of her country chanted a wild lament, as a farewell to her beloved isles: "O heaven! O earth! O mountains! O sea! O my counsellors and my subjects, farewell! O thou land for which my father suffered, the object for which he toiled, we now leave thy shore! Yet will I never disregard thy voice; I will walk by the command thou hast given me."

Then she beckoned to the multitude to be still; and when silence was made, she said, "I am going to a distant land, and perhaps we shall not meet again. Let us pray to Jehovah, that He may preserve us on the water, and you on the shore." Then she called Auna, a Tahitian teacher, and bade him pray. When he had ended his prayer, she waved her hand to the people, and said, "Aloha nui oukou" (great love be with you). As the boat pulled away from the shore, many followed, wading into the water; and these stood waving their hands in sorrowful farewell, and crying "Au-we! au-we!" (alas! alas!), till she had passed away from their sight.

Their bitter foreboding of evil was soon to be realised.

On the 22d May 1824, the Hawaiian party was landed at Portsmouth. A few days later, they appeared in London in somewhat fanciful attire; whereupon tailors and dressmakers took possession of them, and soon equipped them in the height of fashion—and very uncomfortable they must have been! Imagine the ample proportions of a Hawaiian chiefess suddenly confined in the tight-fitting corsets and narrow skirts of the period! They were made the lions of the hour, feasted and flattered, and hurried through a course of sight-seeing and gaieties truly exhausting to these easy-going children of the tropics.

On the 12th of June one of the party was attacked by measles,[1] and within a week all were alike stricken. At first the king gave promise of a fair recovery, but the queen was in danger from the beginning. On the 8th of July she died, and the king, heart-broken, had a serious relapse, and sank

---

[1] This disease, so simple to the British constitution, seems terribly fatal to the races of the Pacific. Witness the introduction to Fiji, in 1875, of one case, so mild as to have rendered quarantine a seemingly unnecessary precaution, but which resulted in the death of 40,000 persons—one-fourth of the whole population.

Again, in the Loyalty group, it carried off one-fifth of the population.—See 'At Home in Fiji.' By C. F. Gordon Cumming. Vol. i. p. 60.

In like manner we can scarcely understand the possibility of men dying of the mumps, but when accidentally introduced to Honolulu in 1839, they spread rapidly all over the isle of Oahu, and thence passed through the whole group. Old and young, strong and weak, were alike affected by them, and a large number of persons died in consequence of exposure and lack of care when the disease seemed to be passing off.

In 1848, measles appeared in the group, spreading rapidly, and with such virulence as to carry off 10,000 persons—that was, one-tenth of the whole population.

That smallpox should have proved a cruel scourge seems more natural. This terrible disease visited Hawaii in 1853, and ravaged certain districts. Thus, in Ewa, in the isle of Oahu, out of a population of less than 3000, 1200 perished; and the living were scarcely able to bury the dead, still less to tend the sick, who lay helpless on the ground, destitute of every comfort. The poor sufferers, totally ignorant of the nature of the new plague, and only seeking a remedy for their burning fever and thirst, plunged into the nearest water—whether sea or stream—and of course suppressed the eruption, causing speedy death. Upwards of 3000 persons died from this cause.

rapidly. On the 14th, he too breathed his last, at the early age of twenty-seven: the queen was a year younger.

Thus ended the long journey, without their having even accomplished the personal interview with George IV., for which they had risked so much. His Majesty, however, granted an audience to the survivors, at Windsor, on the 11th September, when he promised them protection, should any Power attempt to encroach on their independence.

England paid what honour she could to these royal dead. H.M.S. Blonde, a frigate commanded by Lord Byron, was appointed to convey their bodies back to the isles, where they arrived in May 1825. Bitter were the wailings of the people when the terrible news became known. The coffins were carried ashore, and placed on two cars; each was dragged to the chapel by forty of the inferior chiefs, while the air resounded with clamorous lamentations. Yet in their woe the people remembered the lessons taught them by their young queen, and by the king's mother; and instead of renewing heathen rites, they appointed a set time of fourteen days, during which all ordinary pursuits were to be suspended, that the nation might humble itself before the Most High God. The church was thronged, and the voice of mourning was mingled with thanksgiving for the safe return of many friends.

The king's young brother, Kauikeouli, only nine years of age, was then proclaimed king; the chiefs did homage to him, and Kalanimoku, a venerable and much-revered chief, was appointed to govern during his minority, in concert with the queen-dowager, Kaahumanu.

At the council of chiefs held on this occasion, those who had returned from England reported King George's counsel with respect to the American missionaries. They had asked him "whether it was wise to encourage teachers of religion?" to which he had replied, "Yes. They are a people to make others good. I always have some of them by me." He also told them of the former barbarous state of Britain, and referred to its present condition as a proof of what Christianity and civilisation could accomplish.

The chiefs in council then resolved to enact various laws for the good of the country, and to endeavour with a strong hand to suppress the prominent vices of the nation—murder, theft, and excessive immorality. Infanticide was declared to be murder, and subject to the same punishment—namely, banishment. The marriage of near relations was also forbidden. The chiefs had already agreed to recognise the Sabbath, and to adopt the

Ten Commandments as their basis of government.

They received helpful sympathy and good counsel from Lord Byron (H.M.S. Blonde), who made himself much respected, and by whose example the hands of the missionaries were greatly strengthened.

After his departure, however, the rowdy whites strained every nerve to counteract all measures tending to order; the characters of the missionaries were assailed by the grossest calumnies, and every device was tried to shake the faith and good resolutions of the converts.

Hearing that copies of the Ten Commandments were about to be printed in Hawaiian, and freely circulated among the people, these men forced their way to the presence of the king, and by violence and menaces so intimidated the chiefs, that the intention was abandoned.

But the most violent antagonism was shown by the captains and crews of English and American ships, who resented the chiefs' new law prohibiting the brown mermaids from swimming off to the vessels in harbour. Very naturally attributing this reform to missionary influence, many vowed revenge; and but for the interference of the natives, they would assuredly have carried out their purpose of destruction.

The mission-houses at Lahaina and Honolulu

were repeatedly threatened. The former was first attacked by ruffians from the British whale-ship Daniel, who announced their intention of murdering not only the Rev. —— Richards, but also his wife and children, unless the law was repealed. Mrs Richards, though very ill at the time, went out in person to face these scoundrels, and by her brave undaunted bearing so abashed them, that they slunk off muttering oaths and curses. Next morning, however, a boat put off from the ship, flying a black flag, and a large company of sailors (one account says forty men) marched up to the house, armed with knives and pistols. Happily a strong body of natives had assembled, armed with clubs, and forced them to retire. This self-constituted guard remained on duty all the time the Daniel was in port.

Some months later, the crews of several vessels lying off Lahaina declared their determination to murder Mr Richards. They accordingly proceeded to his house, and finding him absent, attempted to demolish it, but again the natives came to the rescue; so the sailors took vengeance by pillaging the town, whence all the women had fled to the mountains.

A year later, a somewhat similar scene was enacted by the John Palmer, another English whaler, and the family of Mr Richards had to take refuge in the cellars from the cannon-balls fired from the vessel as her pleasant parting salute.

In the same way the mission-house at Honolulu was repeatedly attacked by parties of armed sailors, sometimes headed by officers; but in every case the natives rallied to the rescue, and defended their teachers against their white enemies.

But the most cruel outrage was inflicted by a vessel from which these American subjects felt they were most entitled to support,—namely, an armed schooner of the United States—the Dolphin—commanded by Lieutenant Percival. On her arrival at Honolulu, Mr Percival demanded the repeal of the laws, openly threatening to shoot the Rev. Mr Bingham should he appear as interpreter for the chiefs, and also declaring that he would pull down the mission-houses.

On Sunday afternoon, while Mr Bingham was holding service in the house of the regent, Kalanimoku, who was ill, a body of armed sailors from the Dolphin burst into the room, and crowded round the couch of the venerable chief with the usual demands. Much damage was done to the house ere they could be ejected, whereupon, having been joined by a reinforcement from the ship, they made their way to the mission-house. A large body of natives had by this time assembled, and succeeded in driving off the assailants. Urged by their chiefs and teachers, the Hawaiians showed extraordinary forbearance, so that happily no lives were sacrificed.

So far from expressing any regret at this outrage, Mr Percival came ashore in the evening to interview the chiefs, and express his determination not to leave Honolulu till the laws had been repealed. Wearied by his importunity and terrified by his threats, some of the minor chiefs (the regent being very ill) grew fainter in their negatives, and so far yielded, that the party of misrule claimed victory, which they announced with shouts of triumph, and for the ten weeks that this armed vessel remained in port all the old evil customs were revived. Mr Percival was pleased to express to the chiefs his satisfaction at this triumph of might *versus* right, and announced his intention of visiting the isles of Maui and Hawaii, and compelling them also to break through their innovations. To this day the Dolphin is remembered in the annals of Hawaii as the mischief-making man-of-war!

Of course, the example thus set was not lost upon the two thousand seamen who visited Honolulu in the next few months.

Grievous to say, all the chiefs' efforts for good were violently opposed by Mr Charlton, the British consul, who took the part of leader of the opposition, affirming that the Hawaiian rulers had no right to make laws for themselves without first obtaining the sanction of England, and threatening the chiefs with summary vengeance whenever they had occasion to enforce them. Throughout his term of office, from the time of his arrival in 1825, till he happily saw fit to depart in 1842, he never ceased to vex the Mission and the native Government by opposing every scheme for the national good.

It was vain for the chiefs to quote Lord Byron's words, assuring them that England recognised the Hawaiians as a free and independent people, and would in nowise dictate or interfere in their domestic affairs. Mr Charlton chose constantly to assert the supremacy of Great Britain, and his own individual right to exemption from any law. It certainly was not complimentary to Britain to describe her as antagonistic to every effort for good.

Happily all influences were not evil. Eight months after the disastrous visit of the Dolphin, there came another American war-ship—the Peacock—commanded by Captain Jones, a man of a very different stamp. He found a strong body of the most influential foreign residents and ship-masters, headed by the English consul, forming a party systematically hostile to the Christian chiefs, who composed the native Government. They spared no pains in endeavouring to corrupt the converts, whose singularly consistent lives put to shame the

conduct of " civilised " men. So virulent were the accusations they circulated against the missionaries, their system, their politics, that the latter demanded an investigation before Captain Jones and his officers.

The result, in the words of the latter, was the " most complete and triumphant victory that could have been asked by the most devoted friends of the Mission. Not one *iota* derogatory to their character as men or as ministers of the Gospel of the strictest order, could be made to appear by the united efforts of all who conspired against them."[1]

In October 1829, the chiefs plucked up sufficient determination to enact a new criminal code, which they declared should be enforced against foreign residents, as well as against natives. This produced a fresh ferment among the foreign evil-doers, more especially as Mr Charlton was one of those fined for riotous conduct.

Most opportunely, just one week after these laws had been proclaimed, the United States war-sloop Vincennes, commanded by Captain Finch, arrived in harbour on a special mission from the President to the King of Hawaii. Its object was to endeavour to counteract the mischief done by the Dolphin, whose commander had been duly reprimanded. The President's letter to the king stated plainly

[1] Jarves's History of Hawaii, 1843.

that "any American citizen violating Hawaiian law, or interfering with Hawaiian regulation, was offending against his own Government, and worthy of censure and punishment."

Thus happily were the hands of the Government strengthened in dealing with American subjects. As regarded those of England, the course was by no means smooth sailing.

CHAPTER XVIII.

GRADUAL WORKING OF THE CHRISTIAN LEAVEN — "THE IRON CABLE"— KAPIOLANI DEFIES THE GODDESS OF THE VOLCANO — A TIGER-LIKE CONVERT — HOW THE COLLEGE WAS BUILT — TEMPERANCE LEAGUE — BAD FOREIGN INFLUENCE — SCHOOLS FOR GIRLS.

WHILE the work of the Mission was thus hindered and injured by nominal Christians, it was quietly but steadily making way throughout the group. As the *menenia* grass creeps silently and invisibly along the surface of the dry volcanic soil, only revealing its presence when the refreshing dews or rain-showers call it into fulness of life, and from the dry wiry network which overspreads the hills, up-springs the rich crop of sweet green pasture—so the good influence extended insensibly among the people; while in every isle some were found to whom the message of the Gospel proved a life-giving reality.

Among the most notable converts was the queen-regent, Kaahumanu, who was the first to welcome the new-comers, though by no means ready to accept their teaching. By birth the highest chiefess in the isles, she was noted as a cruel, haughty, and imperious woman. Her personal presence was commanding; she was tall and portly, and her carriage queen-like and dignified. Her people held her in fear and reverence, and fell prostrate on the ground as she passed. There was not a man in the isles, however high his station, who dared to face her frown, for the wrath of Kaahumanu carried sentence of death.

Shortly after the death of the great Kamehameha, who was her first husband, she bestowed that post of honour on Kaumualii, King of Kauai, and also on his eldest son, Kealiiahonui—the combined relations of wife and stepmother being strictly in accordance with Hawaiian notions of propriety. Poor Kaumualii had been treacherously captured by King Liho Liho, and brought to Honolulu as a State prisoner. Thus he had been forcibly separated from his beloved wife Kapuli; and though, after his marriage to the queen-regent, he was allowed to return as governor to his own isle, we only hear of poor Kapuli as the loyal chiefess who prevented the islanders from revolting. Kaumualii was, from the first, cordially disposed to the Mission, as his son was one of the young men educated at the Boston College, and brought to Hawaii by the first missionaries.

But the conduct of Kaahumanu towards them was at first cold and contemptuous. Ere long, however, a severe illness greatly softened her character, and she became cordial and friendly to them, especially to Mr Bingham—or Biname, as the natives called him. At the age of fifty she determined to learn to read and write, though her time was fully occupied with the cares of the Government. Two years later, this proud ruler took her place among her subjects at a school examination, as the best example she could give them.

Thenceforward her character was marked by extreme gentleness and kindness; and she was so earnest in promoting the schools, and in herself travelling officially about the isles, exhorting the people to abandon evil ways, and to live conformably to the law of Christ, that they called her Kaahumanu-ho-u, " the new Kaahumanu." They could scarcely believe that it was indeed their once haughty queen who now moved among them so affectionately, giving them her *aloha* (love), and urging them to accept the message of divine love which filled her own heart.

Yet, in dealing with evil-doers, and in enforcing the laws for the good of her people, she showed herself to the last a strong-handed and energetic queen.

Chiefly to her influence was due the downfall of

idolatry; and before she had any thought of joining the Christians, she made a grand tour through Hawaii, searching out and destroying such idols as the people had hidden in caves. Upwards of a hundred were thus collected and committed to the flames, in accordance with the edict that had been pronounced against idolatry.

The people were accustomed to render such implicit obedience to their chiefs, that when these desired them to give ear to the teaching of the new priests, to learn their wonderful arts of reading and writing, to build schools or even churches, they did so without hesitation, and with equal readiness assumed an outward appearance of reformation, which, very naturally, was not more than skin-deep.

With respect to the law for the observance of the Sabbath-day, nothing could have been more entirely in accordance with their national customs, in regard to seasons of *tabu*, when they were required to abstain from all manner of work. The strictest sect of the Pharisees, who would not *themselves* so much as light a lamp on the Sabbath, had their counterpart in the priests and chiefs of the Pacific, who, during seasons of *tabu*, might not feed themselves, but had their food put into their mouths by less scrupulous attendants.

When the noble old queen carried her message

in person, her own intense earnestness doubtless carried considerable additional weight. But the fact that attendance at school and chapel was at first simply an act of national obedience (combined with the extreme caution adopted by the missionaries in admitting converts to Church privileges), accounts for the curious fact that eight years after their arrival in the islands, when the number of white missionaries had been increased to 32, and they had trained 440 native teachers, and counted 26,000 pupils in their schools, and 12,000 attendants at Sunday services, they only numbered 50 native members of the Church—that is to say, baptised persons.

Yet at this very time it is recorded of one village—Lahaina—that it numbered fully fifty homes in which there were family prayers morning and evening; and the resident missionary, Mr Richards, stated that there was scarcely an hour in the day in which persons did not come to ask for individual instruction. Often when he awoke, he found several waiting at his door. Precisely similar was the experience in other districts.

In 1825, Mr Bishop made a preaching tour all round the great isle of Hawaii, a circuit of 300 miles, much of which had to be performed on foot, —now climbing dangerous steeps, then descending into lovely valleys in search of native villages—then skirting the coast in a frail canoe, and again landing to make his difficult way over the rough lava-beds, and across deep gulches and swollen streams.

The journey occupied a month. He found that the people not only crowded to hear him (which they would of course do from curiosity), but that wherever a native teacher had established himself, the people met regularly for worship, abstained from all manner of work or diversion on the Sabbath, and flocked to the school to learn what little the teacher knew. The most remarkable change of all was, that on his whole tour he only saw one man drunk; whereas, only two years previously, Mr Ellis, travelling over the same ground, repeatedly found all the people of a village intoxicated.

One of the earliest to embrace Christianity was the high chief Kalanimoku, who was left guardian of the young prince when his royal brother started on his fatal journey to England. So great was the veneration in which he was held, that the people called him "the Iron Cable of Hawaii." Many a hardly-contested battle had he fought, first in opposition to the great Kamehameha, and afterwards by his side. He had witnessed the first coming of white men—he had aided in the overthrow of idolatry. Now, when the new and holy faith was made known to him, he received and cherished it, and it grew up within his heart, as a tree bearing fruit a thousandfold. The old warrior saw, in his advanced age, only a reason for not losing a day in learning all he could. "I am growing old," he said; "my eyes are dim—I may soon be blind. I must learn in haste, or never know the right way. Come, therefore, to my house, and teach me, for soon my eyes will see no more."

Yet for two years was this aged and earnest disciple kept on probation ere he was admitted to the full communion of the Church. The missionaries were so very much afraid of backsliding on the part of the converts, that their baptism was often delayed for what would seem to us unreasonable periods, of four or five years.

During the short interval of life that remained, "the Iron Cable" threw his whole influence and energy into establishing the government on a Christian footing, bringing up the young king in a right way, and endeavouring to counteract the mischief done by foreigners. In the year 1827 he died, and though all heathen customs were vetoed at his funeral, his stone house, which was the best built in the isles, was dismantled, in accordance with an old superstition. It was customary, on the death of a high chief, to destroy much of his property, lest any survivor should enjoy it. Hence loads of rich satins, velvets, and broadcloth, purchased in exchange for cargoes of sandal-wood, were sometimes carried to the shore, cut into shreds, and cast into the sea.

Here, as in Tahiti, cast-off clothes were sunk in the deep sea to prevent their falling into the hands of sorcerers, who, if they could gain possession of anything that had actually touched a person, were then able to "pray him to death." One of the last heathen sacrifices was offered on Hawaii by the young Princess Kinau, at the instigation of Wahinepio, the sister of "the Iron Cable," for this reason :—

A bundle of her cast-off clothes had been thus sunk in the sea, but it was suspected that one garment had been abstracted by a sorcerer, and there was no knowing what mischief might ensue. So, just to avert possible evil, these ladies determined to make the accustomed heathen offering. But as the village of Lahaina, in which they then were, was a strong centre of Christian work, they supposed the influence of the new faith might annul the efficiency of their sacrifice, so they went secretly to a quiet village eight miles off, where they supposed the old gods might still rule.

Among the most earnest of the converts was Kapiolani, a high chiefess of Kaavaroa, a large district in southern Hawaii. Becoming thoroughly convinced of the truth of Christianity, she commenced by reforming her own life according to its tenets, and did her utmost to promote it among her people. First she abjured somewhat intemperate habits, and became strictly sober; then she dismissed all her husbands except Naihé, who agreed to do all in his power to help her in suppressing all manner of crime, and to awaken the people to an interest in the new faith.

But their task was one of peculiar difficulty. Since the days of Captain Cook, the district had rarely been visited by foreigners; so there had been nothing to shake the reverent awe with which the people continued to worship the dread gods of the great volcano, whose priests and priestesses continued to offer daily sacrifices.

Sometimes these prophets of the volcano-gods went on pilgrimage to other isles, preaching to the people that they should repent of their apostasy, and return to the gods of their ancestors, lest Pélé should overwhelm the isles in her wrath. Many heard these messages with trembling, but generally some one present was able to turn the tide of feeling. For instance, in 1824, the people of Maui were greatly moved by the arrival of a priestess of Pélé—a woman of great stature and haughty bearing, with long black dishevelled hair floating on her shoulders, and a fierce forbidding countenance. She carried in her hand the spear and feather *kahilis* of the goddess. A great multitude followed her, expecting to behold some terrible display of power.

But when she reached the presence of Hoapili-wahine (*i.e.*, the wife of Hoapili), sister to the great Queen Kaahumanu, and heard her strong convincing words, the poor priestess confessed that she had herself been deceiving and deceived. Then, when the Christians present joined in prayer to Jehovah, the priestess threw her *kahilis* (symbols of her office) into the fire, and all the people shouted, "Strong is the *pala pala!*"

But on Hawaii, where the power of the great active volcano is an ever-present reality, nothing had as yet occurred to shake the deep-seated superstition of the people. It was true that, in 1823, the Rev. W. Ellis and his companions had visited the crater, and had eaten the *ohelo* berries sacred to Pélé, without first casting a cluster over the precipice as an offering to the goddess, and had otherwise infringed *tabu*; and yet, no judgment had overtaken them. But then, they were foreigners, and the impunity of their impious conduct had little weight.

So, two years later, Kapiolani determined that she would in person brave whatever danger there might be in defying the fire-gods. Her husband, Naihé, who as yet was only half convinced, entreated her to abstain from this rash deed. All her friends and followers added their petition that she would give up an act of such impious folly. She replied that now all *tabus* alike were done away—that Hawaiians as well as foreigners were all in the safe keeping of the One Great God, and that no power of earth or of hell could harm His servants. So, when they found that she would not be dissuaded, eighty persons determined to bear her company.

She resolved to visit Hilo, where a mission-station had just been commenced; and knowing well how she would strengthen the hands of the teachers, could she in anywise shake the belief of the people in the power of the fire-gods, she resolved to take the mountain-track right across the isle—a distance of upwards of a hundred miles—crossing rugged lava-beds, and involving great fatigue. It was a toilsome pilgrimage, and one which could only be made on foot—for as yet the present passion for riding had not been developed.

From far and near the people assembled in crowds, to implore their beloved chiefess to turn back, and not be so mad as to defy Pélé; but strong in her faith in the protecting power of the God whom she now worshipped, she walked calmly on, encouraging her trembling followers by her brave, trustful words and example. To all who came entreating her to go back, she gave answer, "If I am destroyed, you may all believe in Pélé; but if I am not, then you must all turn to the *pala pala.*"

Kapiolani was better versed in the Scriptures than any other Hawaiian convert. It may be that she drew strength and confidence from the remembrance of that grand Hebrew prophet who, "very jealous for the Lord his God," did not fear to summon the eight hundred and fifty false prophets to meet him on Mount Carmel, that they might offer their sacrifice to Baal, while he alone called on the God of Israel. He, too, bade the people judge according to this test: "If the Lord be God, follow Him: but if Baal, then follow him."

In all the history of the Church, no two scenes occur, so thrilling and so picturesque, as these two champions of the faith (each striking types of Eastern races), standing alone—the one on the green mountains of Judah, the other on the pathway of volcanic fire—to convince the people that the gods whom they all worshipped were, in truth, no gods, and that only one Lord God Omnipotent reigneth!

As Kapiolani drew near to the crater, a prophetess of Pélé came to meet her, and warn her that she was going on to certain destruction. Kapiolani replied that, if she were indeed a prophetess, she must be wise, and could teach her; so she bade her sit down beside her. The woman held in her hand a piece of white bark-cloth, which, she said, was a letter from Pélé. When desired to read it, she held up the cloth, and poured forth a torrent of unintelligible sounds, which she declared to be the ancient sacred dialect.

Then said Kapiolani, "You have pretended to deliver a message from your god, which none of us can understand. I too have a *pala pala*, and will read you a message from our God, which you can understand." She read passages from the Scriptures, telling of the character and works of the true God, and of the Saviour. Then the prophetess hung her head, and said her god had forsaken her, and she could answer nothing.

Elijah slew the prophets of Baal; but the prophets of Pélé were converted by the more loving apostles of the New Covenant, and some became zealous preachers of the Gospel.

On reaching the edge of the crater, Kapiolani led the way to the steep path leading down the side of the precipice to the black lava-bed. All round the crater and along the path the refreshing *ohelo*-berries grow thickly; but no Hawaiian dared taste one till, having gathered a laden branch, he broke it in two, and threw half towards the fiery lake, uttering the accustomed formula, "Pélé, here are your *ohelos*. I offer some to you; some I also eat,"—a form of saying grace which entitled him to eat to his heart's content.

Kapiolani halted, and deliberately ate the berries without this acknowledgment; but her followers dared not do so. After this act of defiance, she descended into the crater, and boldly walked across the great expanse of cooled lava till she reached the brink of the Halemaumau ("the house of everlasting burning"); and as the fiery waves tossed and writhed, she threw broken fragments of lava into the seething mass. A more complete act of desecration could not have been devised.

Then (turning to the followers, who watched her in fear and trembling—half believing that the insulted fire-spirits would take visible form to avenge this insult) she spoke, and her calm, grave words were clearly heard above the hissing and surging of the fiery waves, and remained for evermore engraven on the memory of all present: "My God is Jehovah. He it was who kindled these fires. I do not fear Pélé. Should I perish by her anger, then you may fear her power. But if Jehovah save me while breaking her *tabus*, then you must fear and love Him. The gods of Hawaii are vain."

Then she bade her followers kneel and join with her in a solemn act of adoration of the almighty Creator; and after that, they sang a hymn of praise, that so this, the very home of the fire-gods, might be consecrated as a temple of the Most High.

Then they returned by the way they came, across the undulating sea of hollow lava-waves; and well we may believe how many among them started in terror every time the thin crust gave way beneath their tread, and how often they looked back to see if the dark cloud of sulphureous vapour which slew the foes of Kamehameha, was not arising from the lake to pursue and overwhelm them all. But the blue heaven remained unclouded; and when they had climbed the crater-wall in safety, and turned their faces towards Hilo, they breathed more freely, and felt that the dominion of Pélé was indeed tottering to its fall.

It was a grand, brave deed, and one which carried great weight and bore much fruit, though of course it could not be expected that such a very reasonable and suggestive form of nature-worship should quickly be abandoned. In fact, traces of it still occasionally crop up, much as certain customs of the old fire-worship of Britain linger among ourselves.[1]

Among the remarkable converts at this period was a man who had been formerly employed to catch human victims for sacrifice, and had acquired

[1] For traces of fire-worship in Britain, see 'From the Hebrides to the Himalayas' (C. F. Gordon-Cumming), vol. i. pp. 220-255.

such tiger-like skill in springing on his unguarded prey, that he could actually break the bones of his victim. This purveyor for the heathen altars now came forward to learn the new commandment, and its lesson of loving-kindness.

Schools were now opened in all the principal districts, and in several places churches were built, and large congregations assembled to hear about the new religion. That which was built at Kailua soon proved too small to contain all who wished to hear; so the chief sent his people to the mountains to cut timber sufficient for a very large church. Great was the work involved; and for some weeks several thousand natives worked like a swarm of bees to complete the new building,—hewing and dragging timber, building, cutting grass, and thatching. By the end of the summer, a church, 180 feet by 78, was completed, with room for 4000 people; and not a vacant corner was to be seen on the day of dedication.

Large congregations were a noteworthy feature of this period. At a great meeting of chiefs at Kawaihae, Mr Bishop twice preached to an assemblage of upwards of 10,000 people!

The great church at Kailua was often filled to overflowing on Sunday mornings. People came from distances of seven or eight miles, returning home at night. Those living on the sea-coast came by canoe; and these were drawn up all along the beach during the hours of service. Out of this vast congregation, only twenty-six persons had, in 1828, been received as members of the Church.

Thirty years later the picturesque wooden and thatched church had been replaced by a more durable one of stone. The congregation had dwindled to a thousand; but of these, six hundred were communicants, and the original twenty-six had all gone to their rest. One curious change to be noted was, that the passion for riding had sprung up; and while the canoes of old days had almost disappeared, fully five hundred horses, tied to the rough lava-blocks, waited near the church for their riders.

By 1828, the four Gospels had been translated into Hawaiian, and from fifteen to twenty thousand copies were in circulation. The translation of the complete Bible was of course an exceedingly laborious task, and was not completed till 1839; but various useful school-books and devotional works were published in the interval; and so eager were the people to acquire the art of reading, that schools were found fairly established in places rarely, if ever, visited by missionaries. On the little isle of Molokai, for instance, where only one had casually landed, it was found that out of a population of five thousand, one thousand had enrolled themselves as scholars, and of these a large number could read.

Within ten years after the establishment of the Mission, there were nine hundred schools in the group; but, of course, the teachers were so little in advance of the scholars, that they could do little more than start them. Hence arose the necessity of a High School, in which the teachers should receive such a course of education as should fit them for their post.

Accordingly, it was determined to start a training institute at Lahaina, on Isle Maui, which should be built by the students themselves. A suitable site was selected on the mountain-slope, watered by a stream, where *taro*-beds could be prepared, and the food-supply be thus assured. Then the students repaired to the mountains, felled trees, hewed them to the proper thickness, yoked themselves to the timbers, and dragged them along the ground. For there were neither sawmills to cut up the trees nor teams to drag them. Coral, to make lime, was carried up from the shore; while fuel, with which to burn the coral, and planks for all carpenter's work —writing-tables, benches, &c.—had to be brought from the mountains, a distance of many miles.

In September 1830 the institute was opened—the Rev. Lorrin Andrews being principal—and twenty-five young men were enrolled as students. Three months later, their number had increased to sixty-seven. Their course of study was to embrace four years.

In various ways a good influence was working steadily. Here, as in our own land, one of the chief enemies to be fought was the Giant Drunkenness. When the missionaries landed in Hawaii, they found the king and most of the high chiefs steeped in drink; and often, as I have already mentioned, on their tours round the isles they found whole villages in which all the people were drunk.

In 1831, a temperance society was formed at Honolulu, when about a thousand persons bound themselves to endeavour to stem the evil. They promised not to distil ardent spirits; not to sell them; not to drink them for pleasure; not to give them to friends or to workmen.

Another great step gained lay in the direction of morality. Polygamy and polyandry were alike declared illegal throughout the kingdom of Hawaii-nei. All connections within "the prohibited degrees" were also declared criminal. The king issued an edict that his people should assort themselves in pairs, and that henceforth all such should be considered man and wife. In short, the paternal Government announced its determination to take a strict supervision of the general morals of the people. Among the converts to Christianity, upwards of two thousand religious marriages were celebrated; and altogether, society began to be fairly organised on a better footing.

Unfortunately, here again the adverse influence of the British consul was strongly exerted in antagonism to the native Government, on the plea that no law enacted without direct sanction from England could be valid. Any reform traceable to the influence of the American missionaries was hateful in his eyes. In common with several other foreigners, he seemed to consider no ploy so amusing as that of cajoling "temperance" natives into drunkenness; and it is said that when he could by no other means induce a reformed drunkard to relapse, he would invite him to his house, and disguise spirits in strong coffee, in order to reawaken the craving—a form of treachery which called forth a withering rebuke from one of the intended victims.

The young king had begun well, and gave promise of sobriety and a good rule; but when the foreigners got about him, and plied him with tempting liquors, he fell, as poor Liho Liho had done before him, and, going on from bad to worse, he yielded to the solicitations of these white men, and issued a proclamation, centring in himself all authority, and taking off almost all legal penalties from crime of any sort.

Thereupon ensued a reaction too horrible to contemplate. The truly faithful Christians could do nothing to stem the tide, and the great mass of half-hearted doubters were swept back into the vortex, when the flood-gates of vice were thrown open by the opposition party. Honolulu, "the centre of civilisation," was naturally the centre of grossest evil; but civil and moral anarchy spread like a plague from isle to isle. Schools were deserted, congregations thinned: in some places, notably at Hilo, in Hawaii, idolatrous worship was resumed. Churches were burned; distilleries set up, to extract fiery spirit from the innocent and insipid fruit of the cactus (prickly-pear), and from the large saccharine root of the Ti-tree (dracæna). The wildest orgies of heathenism ran riot. Meanwhile the king gave himself up to a life of the lowest debauchery in the society of his foreign friends, who boasted that the American missionaries would be sent off by the next English man-of-war that touched the isles.

For some months this terrible state of things continued, till the mass of the people, wearied by their own excesses, became filled with disgust at the condition of the country, and voluntarily returned to their teachers, confessing that they had had enough of wickedness, and desired to return to law and order. The king, too, awoke to a sense of the terrible evil he had brought upon his land, and for some time alternated between repentance and relapses. Finally, in 1834, he again gave sanction to the laws; and though some time must needs elapse ere so wild a tempest could subside into anything like real order and calm, there was nevertheless a very general desire for it.

Thanks to the firm rule of Hoapili, the excellent Governor of Maui, this period of misrule did not affect that isle so severely as it did others. This was greatly due to the rigidly enforced law against the traffic in ardent spirits, the advantages of which no class of the community appreciated more fully than the shipmasters. On one occasion a vessel arrived from Honolulu with rum for sale, whereupon no fewer than eighteen shipmasters petitioned the governor to send her away immediately, which he did.

A petition, signed by three thousand persons, was also presented to the king at Honolulu, praying him to prohibit the distillation and sale of intoxicating drink; and similar petitions were presented by all the other isles. The measure was carried, and worked well.

Great good was also done among the shipping population by the establishment of a branch of the American Seamen's Friendly Society, which had its headquarters at Honolulu, and a branch at Lahaina, where a large number of whaling vessels came annually to refit. Here, instead of the wild rowdyism of former years, the men were now peaceable and well-conducted; and at the services held

BAMBOOS AND BANANAS AT HILO.

by the seamen's chaplain, he sometimes reckoned upwards of a hundred and fifty seamen and a dozen captains of vessels.

The parent society at Boston continued from time to time to send reinforcements to the Hawaiian mission-fields; so that by the year 1837 there were in the isles twenty-seven ordained missionaries and upwards of thirty assistants. These were established at seventeen head-stations, each of which became a centre of healthy influence, and an example of domestic comfort and order, which was not lost on the people.

I use the term "comfort" in its comparative sense. To most of us, the life of these settlers would appear full of hardship. Even in much later days, all necessary stores had to be sent from Boston round Cape Horn, a voyage which sometimes took six months. Clothing, stationery, medicines, flour, rice, and sugar, were oftentimes seriously damaged on the voyage, and the long-looked-for supplies were found to be mouldy and worm-eaten. The precious barrel of flour was often transformed into a solid lump, hard as wood, which had to be hewn in pieces with an axe ere the coveted luxury of something like bread could be prepared.

Then, too, the feeling of isolation must have weighed heavily on them. Eighteen months occasionally elapsed ere they received answers to letters sent from the outlying isles to the United States, and even the families living in the group were so widely scattered that it was rarely possible for them to meet. The only means of communication between the different islands was by means of slow and leaky old schooners, which occasionally went the round of the isles to collect trade, and floated lazily along, time being apparently no object.

A trip from Honolulu to Hilo and back (the total distance being six hundred miles) might very likely involve six weeks of this weary travel,—weeks of dirt and discomfort—sometimes lying becalmed, and rolling heavily beneath a burning sun—sometimes driven by adverse winds, and tempest-tost. These wretched ships were generally crowded with natives, pet pigs, and dogs; and the stuffy little cabins were so filthy, that it was better at any cost to lie on deck, despite of sun or rain, or breaking waves and miserable sea-sickness.

During these years the schools made very marked progress. The teachers trained in the seminary at Lahaina were scattered over the isles, and proved more competent than could reasonably have been expected. About 14,000 pupils placed themselves under their instruction. At Hilo, Mr Lyman commenced a boarding-school, with ninety pupils, as preparatory to the Training Institute at Lahaina.

But one of the chief anxieties was the training of girls, so as to raise them, if possible, above the very low standard of morality which seems rooted in the nature of the people. To this end a boarding-school for native girls was opened at Hilo by Mrs Coan, who, with her husband, the Rev. Titus Coan, had arrived in 1835.

As soon as the idea was suggested to the people, they cheerfully agreed to provide food and lodging for twenty girls. Right willingly they worked. Timber was brought from the mountain, grass for thatching from the shore; the men built the house; the women contributed pieces of bark-cloth, mats, bowls, and other useful things. They divided the country round into five districts, each of which undertook in rotation to supply food for the scholars; and every Wednesday, when the people assembled for their weekly meeting, the people of one district brought their offering. One brought a single fish, another a sweet potato, a third a yam or a *taro*, or a piece of sugar-cane. And so a pile was raised which amply provided for the simple fare of the twenty girls.

Mrs Coan was assisted in her labour of love by two carefully trained native women; and soon the school became the ideal home of a company of contented, bright-faced little maidens, docile, industrious, and affectionate. Those who in their own homes had learnt little that was edifying, were now taught to read and write, to sew and braid, to count and to sing, and their lessons were made a pleasure.

Geography, and wonders of far lands, and of natural history, were also taught; and in time of recreation the girls had charge of a delightful garden, through which flowed a pleasant streamlet, affording a cool bathing-place. The children weeded the flower-beds (each girl having charge of one portion), and all kept the gravelled paths neat; while, for their playground, they had a shrubbery of beautiful flowering-plants and fruit-trees—mimosa, mulberry, mango, guava, tamarind, fig, lemon, coffee. No wonder those school-girls loved their happy home at Hilo.

About the same time another school, on a larger scale, was opened at Wailuku, on the island of Maui, where American ladies devoted themselves to instructing fifty girls and women in the arts of sewing, carding, spinning, knitting, and weaving the cotton grown on the isles, and such domestic arts as might tend to home happiness. Those who visited that large family of bright happy girls spoke with amazement of the good that had already been effected, and the love they seemed to bear to one another, and to their teachers.

The school was afterwards enlarged, and only

the want of funds prevented the opening of similar schools in other parts of the isles.

Nor was the industrial education of the men neglected. Although certain white settlers objected to instruct the natives, "lest they should know too much," and even formed a sort of trades-union to prevent their acquiring civilised arts, some of the mission-helpers were able to teach them useful trades, and so enabled them to become creditable workmen in various branches, as carpenters, masons, blacksmiths, tailors, shoemakers, printers, and bookbinders. Altogether, the progress made was satisfactory, notwithstanding all drawbacks.

CHAPTER XIX.

THE GREAT AWAKENING.

One of the most remarkable eras in the story of Hawaii occurred between the years 1837 and 1843. It is known, in the story of the Mission, as "the great awakening," and was, in fact, a very wonderful wave of religious influence which swept over the whole land, so that from every corner of the group came accounts of what we should call great revival-meetings.

It was like an electric thrill affecting all the isles, especially Oahu, Maui, and Hawaii. On the latter, the resident clergy had been absent visiting the distant schools. Their canoe was wrecked, and they had just managed to swim ashore, when a message was brought to them from the mission-house at Kaawaloa, bidding them return at once, for "strange things were happening—the natives were coming in companies, asking what they should do to be saved."

They returned to find that from morning till night, and almost from night till morning, the house was besieged by crowds, who patiently waited their turn to have a personal talk with the men who could teach them the right way. For weeks and months this continued, and the missionaries could scarcely secure time for needful sleep and food. Many who lived at distances of fifty and sixty miles came regularly to attend the Sunday services, devoting the whole of Saturday and Monday to travelling to and fro.

At that one station the names of upwards of two thousand persons were noted as anxious inquirers after the truth, and there was good reason to believe that many were thoroughly in earnest. But all were kept in training-classes for at least a year, and then were only admitted to baptism after the most strict examination.

In 1838, news was received simultaneously from all parts of the isles that the interest awakened was such that the people seemed to think of nothing else. Those who hitherto had been the most dull and stupid, and those who had not a thought beyond the lowest pleasures, were now roused to self-examination and prayer. Their favourite sins were forsaken. Those who had hitherto turned a deaf ear to every lesson of holiness, now came, as meek penitents, resolved to begin a new life; and their friends and companions declared that the change was no outward show, but a great reality. On Sundays and week-days the churches were crowded; and so great were the congregations which assembled, that although the churches were for the most part large airy buildings, they could not contain the multitudes, who had either to assemble in relays, or to hold great camp-meetings in the open air.

Honolulu was divided into two congregations—one of considerably over 2000, the other numbering nearly 4000. At Wailuku, on Maui, there were nearly 2000; at Ewa, on Oahu, 4000.

At Lahaina, which was one of the chief shipping-stations, and a place where the Mission had long been established, the teachers marvelled to see hardened old heathens, on whom they had for fifteen years vainly striven to make any impression, now coming forward of their own accord—some leading others. Blind men, who had never before entered the church, now bade some child guide them thither; poor cripples crawled painfully on hands and knees to every meeting, and sat drinking in the good words they heard, as though to them they were truly words of life.

The women had prayer-meetings among themselves; but the most remarkable feature of the awakening in Lahaina was the spirit of devotion which seemed to have been outpoured on the children—poor neglected little ones, thoroughly versed in all the sins of their elders, both of native growth and foreign importation. Now it seemed as if the Saviour's invitation to "the little children" had been whispered to them all—for the rudest and roughest became the gentlest and most docile, and the noise of boisterous mirth on the beach was hushed, for the children seemed irresistibly drawn to the banana and sugar-cane groves, where many a time their wondering parents found them kneeling and praying, in all the earnest, simple faith of childhood.

On the island of Molokai (which is now converted into that saddest of colonies—a leper-station), the resident missionary noted the first indication of an awakening among his people, by remarking that a considerable number commenced to assemble in the schoolhouse an hour before dawn, to plead that God would send His Holy Spirit among them. Nor was their prayer unanswered. Soon each village on Molokai seemed pervaded with the same great longing; and to all came the same gracious influence, so that it seemed to some who were present as though the blessedness of the first Whitsunday were once more vouchsafed to those expectant disciples who waited for the gift of God.

The story of one island was more or less that of

all. Everywhere there was a disposition to learn, such as had never before been manifested; and the missionaries were not slow to take advantage of this happy state of feeling. Night and day they laboured, striving to reach all. They travelled to the remotest villages, climbing difficult ravines, facing wild storms—visiting, conversing, examining, preaching—in season and out of season. They preached from seven to twenty—sometimes even thirty—times in a week, to hearers who seemed to hang upon their words as though they could never be satisfied.

During these six years, out of a total population of about 130,000, 27,000 persons were admitted to baptism,—never without a long period of probation and free personal intercourse with every candidate, in order, as far as possible, to guard against the danger of mere fashion or of false motives. As a matter of course, out of so great a multitude, who in youth had been heathen savages, a certain number were afterwards reckoned backsliders, according to the exceedingly rigid tests and lines drawn by a Church framed on the straitest principles of the Puritan Fathers of New England. The marvel is, that so large a majority should have stood the test of constant supervision for the next thirty years, without incurring blame from their pastors.

In no district throughout the group was the

awakening so remarkable as at Hilo, on Hawaii. Then, as now, the Rev. Titus Coan and the Rev. Mr Lyman were in charge of the Mission. The former had arrived in the isles in 1835, and had just succeeded in thoroughly mastering the language (which apparently lends itself to the fervid eloquence with which heaven has endowed him, as readily as does his mother-tongue). Being a man of an iron constitution, seemingly incapable of fatigue, and already inured to hardship in his attempt to establish a mission in Patagonia, it was natural that, in the division of work, it should be his part to go forth into the wilderness, like a modern St John the Baptist, preaching repentance, while his less robust coadjutor, Mr Lyman, should remain in charge of the training-school and other work at Hilo.

His nominal flock dwelt in widely scattered villages in the deep glens which seam the rough mountains, extending over an area of a hundred miles; and nowhere in the world, I suppose, is there more exhausting ground to be got over than in climbing up and down the innumerable deep gulches, from twenty to a thousand feet in depth, which lie in the neighbourhood of Hilo. No fewer than sixty-five, at the lowest computation, must be crossed in travelling from Hilo to Lapa-hoe-hoe, a distance of thirty miles; and through each of these rushes a beautiful stream, which in stormy weather becomes a raging torrent, rushing, foaming, and here and there leaping a precipice, and forming cascades, beautiful to the artist, but not altogether pleasant to the pedestrian.

Across these gulches, and through tangled forest, haunted by herds of fierce wild cattle, and often travelling for weary miles over the roughest lava-beds, beneath a blazing sun, this faithful apostle toiled in search of his people, braving storms and floods such as might well have shaken nerves that were not made of iron.

In one of his letters at this time, he thus describes one of his journeys on foot round Hawaii, a distance of three hundred miles: "In order to compass my plans, and reach each village at the time appointed, I was obliged to labour incessantly from morning till night, and sometimes till midnight. Owing to the very heavy rains, the steep and lofty banks of the ravines became slippery, difficult, and dangerous. Many are wellnigh perpendicular, and can only be ascended by climbing with the utmost care, or descended only by letting one's self down from crag to crag by the hands; and in many places the traveller is obliged to wind his way along the sides of a giddy steep, where one step of four inches from the track would plunge him to a fearful depth below. Over these precipices I had often to climb during downpours of rain; and having neither time nor place to change my saturated raiment, I had to stand and preach for one or two hours to a congregation who were already assembled and waiting for me.

"But what rendered this tour truly perilous was the swollen and furious state of the rivers. Their rush was rapid and fearful. Some of them I succeeded in fording, some I swam by the help of a rope made of tough hibiscus fibre, and slung across the stream to prevent me from being swept away by the raging current; and over some I was carried passively on the broad shoulders of a powerful native, who passed safely with me through a strong current up to his arm-pits, while a company of powerful men locked hands, and extended themselves across the stream just below, in order to save me from going over a near cataract in case my bearer should fall. Many of the less hardy and daring of the natives, after several unsuccessful attempts to cross, and after the most hair-breadth escapes from being swept down the cataracts, gave up the struggle, and consented to remain behind."

My own experience of one of these rivers in flood[1] brings the perils of such a journey very vividly to my imagination.

So suddenly do these streams rise, that it some-

[1] See chap. x.

times happened that Mr Coan reached the brink of a rocky ravine to find all calm and peaceful, and while he stood talking to the people, a sound of roaring waters would be heard, which warned him that not a moment was to be lost. Seizing his leaping-pole (a staff eight or ten feet in length), he let himself down the precipitous bank, and sprang from rock to rock, gaining the opposite shore only a moment before the turbid flood rushed down in a wall of tumultuous waters six or eight feet in depth.

His luggage on these occasions was of the simplest order. Two large gourds contained his scanty supplies. In one was stored a change of raiment; in the other, some needful medicines and provisions. One such calabash, with half of another to act as cover, makes a very light and waterproof little box.

His finding large congregations assembled to receive him was due to the fact, that in order to save valuable time, in working among a population so widely scattered, it was sometimes found desirable to send messengers to announce his coming. At all times much valuable work was done by the native converts. Those who were found to be discreet, prayerful, active, and intelligent, were stationed at important posts, with instructions to hold prayer-meetings, sabbath-schools; to visit the sick; to gather in the children; to seek out the wretched and wandering, and bring them to the house of God; and generally to watch over the people. By their influence many of the most wild and uncultivated were tamed and softened, and induced to abandon their evil ways, and turn to the Lord.

Active members of the Church were selected and sent forth, two and two, into every village, to preach the Word. They climbed the mountains, traversed the forests, and explored the glens to seek the outcast and neglected sons of Hawaii. None were neglected. In the same letter from which I have already quoted, Mr Coan says: "The aged and infirm, the blind, halt, and withered, have been sought out, and the Gospel has been preached to them by the wayside and in their homes. Many of these sufferers have been led by the hand; others have been brought in litters, or on the backs of their friends, to the place of worship. On my tours through Hilo and Puna, multitudes of this poor and afflicted class are brought from their scattered homes in the glens, and laid by the wayside, that they may get an interview with the missionary as he passes, and obtain a little balm, not only for the soul, but also for the body."

He adds that he made a point of always carrying medicines with him for this purpose,—no easy matter, considering the nature of the ground over which he travelled.

On all these tours he held protracted meetings at every village, and was in the habit of preaching from twenty to thirty times a-week, in addition to holding ceaseless conversation with individuals. At the close of one such long and fatiguing day, a friend asked him if he did not feel utterly exhausted. His reply was, "A little leg-weary!" He is happily endowed with a throat and lungs which till recently knew no weariness! During one of his tours he preached no less than forty-three times in eight days!

Sometimes he commenced preaching at daybreak, and held three distinct services before he could find leisure so much as to eat. He could not cross the threshold of any house where he might halt, without being thronged by people from all quarters. They stationed themselves in small companies by the wayside, and some followed him for days from village to village to hear the Gospel. It was like the early days of preaching in Judea.

That "the appetite doth grow with that it feeds upon" was certainly true in this case — for the people having tasted of the Water of Life, thirsted for deeper draughts; nor could they rest satisfied with a periodical visit from a native teacher, who, till very recently, had been as ignorant as themselves. So they poured down to Hilo in vast companies, and there built for themselves simple grass-thatched huts, that they might be at hand, and lose no chance of hearing the Word of God. The village, which hitherto had numbered a population of about a thousand, now increased tenfold; yet no difficulties arose — all was quiet and orderly. Their one wish was to learn, and for two years this great camp-meeting was continued—a ceaseless round of classes and services. Of course necessary work was not neglected, and all worked busily at their gardens or their fishing, to supply food for so great a multitude.

The village already possessed a native-built church, capable of accommodating about six thousand persons. The new-comers built a second, large enough to contain three thousand; and at any hour, from the earliest glimmer of dawn onward, it needed but a blast on the trumpet-shell, which acted the part of church-bell, and a congregation assembled large enough to fill both buildings, the people sitting so compactly on the matted floor, that any one looking in would see only a dense forest of heads. One might walk *over* them, but to walk *among* them was often impossible; and though the churches were filled to overflowing, hundreds remained outside who could not find room to enter, but crowded near, trying to hear the Word spoken within.

Here is an account of one of these newly gathered congregations: "It is a sea of heads, with eyes like stars. They are far from being still. There is a strange mingling of the new interest and the old wildness, and the heated mass seethes like a caldron. An effort to sing a hymn is made—to our ears a rude inharmonious song, but an honest attempt, such as God accepts as praise. Prayer is offered, and then comes the sermon. The preacher feels as though he were bound by an electric chord to the restless mass of human beings packed before him. He preaches the grand old truths, and puts them as simply and as plainly as he possibly can; does not try to excite the people; yet soon many tremble and weep, and some cry aloud for mercy."

Many of the wildest and rudest were so overwrought by their own feelings, that they fell down swooning; and when this was reported to the brethren in other districts, they assumed that the preacher had been endeavouring to get up a false excitement, and they bade him check all such manifestations of overwhelming interest. Mr Coan's reply was characteristic.

"How could I put this down?

"I didn't get it up! I didn't believe the devil

would set men to praying, confessing, and breaking off their sins by righteousness. These were the times when thieves brought back what they had stolen. Lost things reappeared, and quarrels were reconciled. The lazy became industrious. Drunkards stopped drinking. Thousands broke their pipes and gave up tobacco (which was used as an intoxicant). Adulteries ceased, and murderers confessed their crimes. Neither the devil nor all the men in the world could have got this up. Why should I put it down? In the Old Testament Church there were times when the weeping of the people was heard afar.

"I always told the natives that such demonstrations were of no account—no evidence of conversion. I advised to quietness. I said, if they were sorry for their sins, God knew it; if they were forgiven, they need not continue to weep. And I especially tried to keep them from hypocrisy.

"Many a time have I blushed, and felt like hiding my face in the dust, when I have witnessed the earnest wrestlings of these natives, and have seen how, like princes, they have had power with God, and have prevailed. They take Him at His word; and with a simple and childlike faith, unspoiled by tradition or vain philosophy, they go with boldness to the throne of grace. With tears, with soul-melting fervour, and with that earnest importunity which takes no denial, they often plead the promises, and receive what appear to be the most direct and unequivocal answers to their prayers."

Naturally, these earnest hearers soon craved to be admitted into the outward and visible Church; and here arose Mr Coan's chief difficulty. His brethren had strongly insisted on terms of probation extending over years. He pleaded the example of the apostles, and the thousands whom they baptised, so soon as the converts declared their faith in the Lord Jesus—though many of these afterwards fell into sin, and some even apostatised. He urged the danger of delay, and its folly, when the work was so unmistakably a holy inspiration. So he resolved to break through the custom of the Mission, and to receive all those of whose sincerity he was well assured, after from six months to a year of careful instruction and personal care, bestowed day by day, and week by week.

The minuteness and order with which this was accomplished seem almost incredible. In all those crowds, there was not one with whom Mr Coan did not make himself personally acquainted, and whose name was not recorded in his private note-book, with such particulars as might keep the individual vividly before his mind. Every time he journeyed through his great parish, all the candidates for baptism were called up by name, and he conversed with each individually — warning, exhorting, or encouraging, as the case seemed to require. Thus the location, life, and feelings of every member of this great flock became a matter of personal knowledge to its pastor, who, week by week, noted the progress of each, while friends and enemies were publicly desired to testify if they knew any just cause or impediment why these persons should not be received into the Church.

First and last, Mr Coan has himself baptised twelve thousand adults and four thousand infants. But the brethren (who would have deemed it blasphemy to question the wisdom of St Peter in baptising three thousand persons on the day of Pentecost, or of Philip in suffering the Ethiopian eunuch to stop his chariot, that he might straightway receive baptism in the nearest pool) were greatly disturbed at hearing of these innovations, and deemed that all Church discipline was endangered.

Again Mr Coan had to stand on his defence. "I can see no good reason," he says, "why, when I had baptised one hundred converts, who, by the confessions of my most discreet brethren, ought to come into the Church, I should not consistently baptise one hundred more, of equally unexceptionable qualifications. When our Church numbered from twenty to fifty cold, halting, doubting professors—when our congregation was less than a thousand on Sabbath mornings, and barely four hundred in the afternoon—when the annual addition to our Church members was five or ten, and the thousands around us were going down to the grave in unbroken columns,—there was no alarm. Whence, then, the present fears? I suppose the great numbers added to our churches is what staggers the faith of many: in fact, a letter received from one, deeply interested in the work, says, 'If there were only a few hundreds, we could believe; but there are so many, it spoils it all'!"

Like many, who read the predictions and promises of the Bible with a kind of romantic rapture, so long as they are supposed to refer only to far-distant glories, these brethren fully believed in the outpouring of the Holy Spirit in apostolic days, and looked for His universal influence on "young men and maidens, old men and children," in some unknown future. But that they should believe in it as a present reality, was a different matter; and that the people thus favoured should be a race of ignorant, despised, half-naked islanders, proved a stumbling-block and an offence to many.

Those who were working on the spot saw it in a very different light. Again I quote from Mr Coan: "I have seen a glorious and overwhelming work of God going on without abatement in Hilo and Puna for more than two years. Some of the precious evidences that God has wrought a good and glorious work among our people, may be seen in their breaking off from old and cherished sins— in their present quiet and peaceable lives, in their searching 'for the word of God, and readiness to receive instruction — in the spirit of grace and supplication poured upon them—in their anxious efforts to save sinners, and their cheerful liberality in good works. Our congregation on the Sabbath averages four thousand, and is nearly as large in the afternoon as in the morning.

"On such special occasions as the celebration of the Lord's Supper, the concourse of people has swelled to seven thousand or more.

"Hitherto all the healthy and strong of the flock have assembled periodically at Hilo for this sacrament; while, for the comfort and edification of the feeble, the sick, and the aged, I have administered this holy rite in different places in distant parts of the isle. The number of communicants who assemble at Hilo is now so great, that we have to divide them into two companies—one half celebrating the Holy Supper in the morning, the other in the afternoon."

One day in the summer of 1838—a day never to be forgotten in the annals of Hilo, or in the history of missions—the first-fruits of this great awakening were gathered into the Church. Upwards of one thousand seven hundred candidates for baptism assembled in the church. All had been resident at the station for many weeks, and no pains had been spared, no tests left untried, to prove that each candidate was a true penitent. Once more, all joined in prayer and singing, and once again a clear explanation was given, lest any should trust in the mere external rite. Then, as they sat or knelt in long rows on the matted floor, Mr Coan and Mr Lyman passed reverently to and fro among the silent multitude, bearing a bowl, from which they sprinkled on each bent head the sacred symbolic waters, after which, to all collectively, were addressed the words, to us familiar from our cradles, to them so new and so full of awe — " I baptise you all, into the Name of the Father, and of the Son, and of the Holy Ghost."

Then the Holy Communion was celebrated, and the newly baptised were admitted to the holy rite, making a total of two thousand four hundred communicants present. It was a crowd of which the poor, the maimed, the halt, and the blind, formed a conspicuous part. " It seemed," said Mr Coan, "like one of the crowds gathered by the Saviour, and over which He pronounced the words of healing. It was a company in which were numbered the old and decrepit, the lame and the blind, the withered, the paralytic,—those who, through their own sins or the sins of their fathers, were afflicted with divers diseases and torments; the depraved and loathsome came hobbling upon their staves, led or carried by their friends, and sat down at the table of the Lord.

"Among them were to be seen the hoary priest of idolatry, with hands but recently, as it were, washed from the blood of human victims, together with the thief, the adulterer, the sorcerer, the robber, the murderer, and the mother (no! the monster!) whose hands have reeked with the blood of her own children. . . . These are the lost whom the Son of Man came to seek and to save. And in very deed He is here present."

It was a company of which there was reason to believe that each had " truly and earnestly repented of their sins, and steadfastly purposed to lead a new life. There was a hush upon the vast crowd without, who pressed about the doors and windows. The candidates and the congregation were all in tears, and the overshadowing presence of God was felt in every heart."

As it may possibly occur to some who are accustomed to think of the consecrated elements of bread and wine as essential to the administration of this holy sacrament, to marvel how such imported luxuries were provided for so great a multitude, I may mention that no such fruitless effort was made. It was judged that as the Master made use of the ordinary daily food of Judea, so would He bless that of Hawaii. Therefore sweet water from the cocoa-nut, or from the sparkling brook, replaced the juice of the grape, while breadfruit or *taro* represented the sacred bread. Even had the foreign elements been procurable, it would have been impossible to prevent the people from attaching superstitious meaning to these unknown dainties.

This great gathering together of the people afforded Mrs Coan and Mrs Lyman a grand opportunity of specially instructing the women, and they made right good use of it. Being the only two white women in Hilo, and tied to their home duties and the care of their little ones, they could never have visited their brown sisters in their scattered villages. But now that ten thousand persons had assembled round their very doors, they laboured night and day to teach them useful domestic arts, such as sewing and plaiting, which resulted in the manufacture of the *holuku* (the loose flowing robe of coloured calico), and in the plaiting and making of the neat little hats, which to this day form the national dress of all Hawaiian (as of all Tahitian) women.

Nor were the children forgotten. Much care

was bestowed on them, to teach them nice habits of neatness and of decency. Mr Coan himself conducted a large Sunday-school, at which an average of five hundred little ones attended; and besides this, there was a weekly lecture for the children, and various classes for their instruction. Here, as at Lahaina and elsewhere, there was good reason to believe that many of these babes had become Christians, in heart and in truth.

Speaking of the "cheerful liberality" of the people, as an evidence of their being in earnest, Mr Coan says: "They are poor, distressingly poor, and not a few of them are themselves the objects of deep commiseration; yet, at the monthly offertory, all stand ready with their 'two mites,' often given out of the deepest poverty. Among these humble gifts, you will see one bring a bunch of hemp, another a piece of wood for fuel, a mat, a *tappa*, a *malo* (*i.e.*, a narrow strip of bark cloth), a little salt, a fish, a fowl, a *taro*, a potato, a cabbage, a little arrowroot, a few ears of corn, a few eggs. The old and feeble, and children, who have nothing else to give, gather grass, wherewith to cover and enrich the soil. Each gives according to his ability, and shuns to approach empty-handed."

During the four years that the great awakening was at its height, 7557 persons were received into the Church at Hilo. This embraced about three-fourths of the entire adult population. After this, they returned to their own homes, and the one huge congregation was divided into seven local, independent churches. These established fifteen places of worship at the principal villages in the district, each of which continued to be a centre of Christian work.

The building of these churches was a very serious undertaking. It was no light task, to be done by hirelings, but a labour of love, in which each individual contributed his own work. If it was to be a native building of timber and thatch, the men went off to the mountains, and sought out the finest trees in the forest. Although native stone-adzes had been replaced by iron, still axes were scarce, and it was not always easy to get them sharpened, so that felling a large tree involved tough work. When this was accomplished, there remained the toil of dragging the huge log to the village, a distance probably of at least a dozen miles. This had to be done by human strength, for horses and cattle had not yet been recognised as helpers, and would, moreover, have been unable to work, because of the deep gulches and precipitous ravines which had to be crossed.

So a great company of men and women—sometimes as many as a hundred and fifty persons of both sexes—harnessed themselves by strong ropes, to the fallen timber, and dragged it by main force across the rough lava-beds, and through the tangled brushwood, up and down steep ravines, and across rivers, and over all the difficult ground, which is so wearisome even to walk on. And as they toiled the livelong day, they chanted wild choruses, to inspirit one another, and help them on their way.

Meanwhile the feebler women, and children, were busy collecting grass or reeds for thatching, and plaiting elaborate fibre-string with which to bind the rafters, or weaving mats for the floor.

If they were ambitious, and wished to build a stone church, such as the foreign teachers recommended, then far greater labour was involved. If there were any old heathen temples in the neighbourhood, they were saved the work of preparing the stones, but had to carry them on their shoulders for long distances. In order to obtain lime, they had to go off to the coral-reef, and dive 10 or even 20 feet below the surface. Then, when they had succeeded in detaching a mass, they fastened a rope to it, and drew it up to their canoe, and then dived for another piece. If they lived inland, they must either carry the coral several miles uphill, or else carry down fuel from the mountains to burn the coral on the beach, and then carry up the lime in aprons of bark cloth, or in calabashes, or empty gourds. And when they had accumulated many barrels of lime, then they had to collect as much sand; and even water had sometimes to be brought from long distances.

If there were no heathen *marais* near to supply stone, and the people were resolved to have a stone church, then they engaged native masons and carpenters, and agreed to pay them with such things as they possessed. On the little island of Molokai, for instance, the women subscribed 200 dollars, which they earned by making mats, each woman earning only eight cents (fourpence) a-week; and the men's contribution was raised by transporting firewood by canoe to Lahaina, a distance of 20 miles. Each canoe-load sold for about 50 cents (two shillings). So, directly or indirectly, every individual of the congregation took an active part in the building of their village sanctuary.

Such churches as the great stone church at Honolulu, and the large church at Hilo, were naturally considered triumphs of architectural skill. The former was erected at a cost of 30,000 dollars, and was dedicated in the year 1842. The church at Hilo cost about 13,000 dollars in money, besides much gratuitous labour. It was completed in 1859, and was built to replace the original big church, which suddenly fell after a heavy rain-storm, the wooden posts having become decayed, and unable to support the weight of soaking thatch.

Once a church was completed, there was no danger of a congregation lacking. No matter how stormy the weather, the people assembled from far and near,—many travelling distances of several miles by rugged and precipitous mountain-tracks, in the pouring, pitiless tropical rain, their scanty cotton garment and their flowing hair alike drenched. And as we may safely assume that their accustomed coating of oil was omitted when the cotton dress came into fashion, it is evident that such soakings must rank among the many causes which have tended so sadly to depopulate the isles.

However, it all tends to prove that the people were in earnest; and so, outwardly, but more especially inwardly, the great work went on; and at the close of 1843 it was found that, in the course of the previous six years, 27,000 people had been received as members of the Christian Church. Out of so vast a number, it was not to be supposed that some would not fall away; for even among our Lord's own apostles, did not one of the twelve prove "a devil"? But the proportion was exceedingly small. After some years, it was found that those who had come under Church censure were but an average of one in sixty; and yet no lax standard was allowed. On the contrary, a most strict and careful supervision of the converts was maintained, and the majority of cases of Church discipline were called forth by such apparently trivial offences as smoking to excess [1]—a crime not unknown in Britain, but one which it was particularly necessary to discourage in Hawaii, as the manner of smoking was such as to produce a form of intoxication; and temperance in all forms was an essential qualification for Church membership.

Nor was it only in the comparative seclusion of their own isles that these men stood firm. Many of them found their way to Oregon and California; and at the time of the great gold-rush, a considerable number went to seek their fortunes at the diggings. But so far from bringing discredit on their Christian profession, they were noted among the roughs of all nations as men who would not drink or gamble, or profane the Sabbath.

Twenty years more passed by, and in 1868 it was computed that 20,000 more Hawaiians had received Christian baptism,—making up a total of about 50,000 persons who had joined the Church since the commencement of the Mission in 1820.

Wonderful indeed was the change wrought in those forty years. A race of most thievish naked savages had been transformed into a community of

---

[1] The annual expenditure on tobacco in its various forms in the British Isles is no less a sum than £16,000,000 sterling.

Britain's annual contribution to foreign missions has for the last ten years been something over £1,000,000. In 1880, it reached £1,108,000.

singularly honest, decently-clothed people. Throughout the isles there was not a cottage which did not possess its Bible and hymn-book, and in which daily family-prayer and the custom of thanksgiving at every meal were not invariable. It would have been hard to find any person who could not read and write, and who had not some knowledge of arithmetic and geography. This fact is the more remarkable (as showing how well the natives had profited by their opportunities in comparison with the whites with whom they had come in contact), because, of all the business documents in the possession of the Hawaiian Government, accumulated in their intercourse with foreigners, one-half bear the *marks* of the latter, who could not even sign their own name!

Now, every village had its own church and school, built by the people at their own cost; and besides 400 common schools, there were several of a higher class both for men and women. The theological and general training-college at Lahaina-luna had already sent forth about 800 trained men, the majority of whom were scattered as teachers all over the isles. Thirty were ordained ministers, and a considerable number had gone forth as missionaries to distant groups, to carry thither the gift they had themselves received. Some were fairly started in secular professions, as surveyors, lawyers, and even judges. In addition to the training-college at Lahaina, a theological school had been commenced by Mr Alexander at Wailuku, and Mr Coan had a similar undertaking at Hilo.

The education of the young chiefs of the highest rank was undertaken by Mr and Mrs Cooke, who received upwards of a dozen at a time as inmates of their own house. To the extreme care bestowed on their culture many in England can testify, who still remember the two young princes, sons of the Princess-Regent Kinau, and grandsons of the great Kamehameha, who visited England in 1849, and who afterwards reigned successively as Kamehameha IV. and V. Another who was for a while the pupil of Mrs Cooke, is the Dowager-Queen Emma, who also, by her grace and goodness, won golden opinions in England, when, widowed and childless, she visited our isles. King Lunalilo, the Well-beloved, and the present King Kalakaua, were also educated in this same home school.

There are not many preceptors who can boast of having educated four kings and a queen!

Another care, which now became prominent, was the education of the missionaries' children, who numbered about 130. Forty missionary families were by this time scattered over the isles, practically teaching the advantages of well-regulated domestic life; and it was considered that it would be highly advantageous to induce them, if possible, to remain permanently in the group.

Certain advantages were accordingly offered to them, and a school was established at Punahou, which eventually developed into the Oahu College, its object being to give such thorough training as to avoid the necessity of sending young men to America. Thus a great inducement was afforded to them to remain permanently in Hawaii, and become colonists; and thus it is that all the early missionaries are represented at the present day by children and grandchildren, who rank as leading citizens.

CHAPTER XX.

THE STORY OF HAWAII'S FOREIGN MISSIONS — THE HAWAIIAN CHURCH DECLARED INDEPENDENT OF AMERICA — PROGRESS OF MORALITY.

FROM the commencement of the Mission till the time when (about A.D. 1863) Hawaii was acknowledged to be a Christian nation, capable of ruling its own Church affairs, the American Board had sent thither 52 ordained missionaries, 21 lay helpers, and 83 female missionaries, married and single.

Of the first-named, 10 died at their posts, after an average of 27 years' work; and sixteen still remain, who have worked in Hawaii from 30 to 50 years—a fact which speaks well for the climate.

The parent Society ruled that the legitimate work of a Missionary Society was accomplished when it had raised up a self-governing, self-sustaining Christian community, imbued with so much spiritual life as would insure the prosecution of its own home missions, and also the existence of such an aggressive tendency as would lead to the prosecution of foreign missions in lands still heathen.

I think it was Bishop Wilberforce who said that zeal for foreign missions, or indifference towards them, affords "a pulse-like index to the spiritual health of Christ's visible body—the Church."

According to this standard, the young Hawaiian Church must be in a truly vigorous state of health. Not only is it entirely self-supporting and self-governed, but one-fourth of the total number of Hawaiians who have been ordained to the ministry are now working as missionaries in various parts of Micronesia and in the Marquesas.

The Hawaiian Society for Foreign Missions was formed at Honolulu in 1850, and, two years later, three missionaries from Boston — Messrs Snow, Gulick, and Sturges—arrived with their wives, on their way to commence work in the utterly savage isles near the equator. The nearest of these was at a distance of 2000 miles from the Sandwich Isles, and the people were known to be fierce and cruel; but seven of the Hawaiian teachers volunteered to join the mission-party. It was only deemed advisable to allow two men, with their wives, to accompany this pioneer-party, but others followed at short intervals.

Their first station was on Kusaie or Strong's Island, the easternmost of the Caroline group, about 500 miles from the Gilbert Isles. The second station was on Ponape, or Ascension Island, one of the same cluster, but 300 miles farther west. Both are singularly beautiful—volcanic masses, with rich soil and good climate. Ascension is described as a little paradise—a high basaltic island, sixty miles in circumference, surrounded by ten smaller basaltic isles, all enclosed within a protecting coral-reef. The mountains rise to about 3000 feet, and rivers and waterfalls lie in the richly-wooded valleys, where stately bread-fruit trees, mango, cocoa-palm, sugar-cane, and many another tree pleasant to the eye and good for food, flourish among noble forest-trees, while twenty varieties of birds give life to the scene. For those who love the tropics, the climate is delightful, the thermometer only ranging seventeen degrees in three years. Everything in the natural surroundings was most attractive, with the usual exception—that "only man is vile;" and very vile they proved here.

However, when the vessel anchored in the land-locked harbour of Ponape, the king came on board, welcomed the strangers, and said it would be "good for them to stop." So they disembarked, and soon discovered a population of about 5000 persons, whose leaf-huts were hidden among the overhanging forests. Here Messrs Sturges, Gulick, Kaaikaula, and their wives, began work; while Mr

Snow and Opunui settled on Kusaie, which is also a mountainous isle, about 2000 feet in height, and wooded to the summit. The population numbered about 1500, and proved singularly attractive. Strange to say, polygamy was unknown, and the manufacture of all intoxicating drinks was strictly prohibited. The new-comers and their message were alike kindly received, and few distractions from the outer world came to interfere with their work. So isolated is the isle, that two years elapsed ere a letter reached them from America.

The good seed took root quickly, but no care could check the strange, sad mortality among the people. In 1869, the report from Kusaie stated the population to be only 600 natives, and not one white man (Mr Snow having gone to a new post in the Marshall Isles). But a native pastor was in charge of the isle, and the people had built for themselves four churches, in which they regularly assembled for worship—in each case conducted by an ordained native minister.

The work at Ponape proved more difficult. In the first six months fifteen vessels called; and though in most cases the captains proved friendly, some were the reverse, and made considerable trouble, while the influence of the sailors was, as usual, most pernicious. One of these vessels brought the smallpox, which carried off a multitude of the inhabitants, and produced a general recklessness and bitterness of feeling among the people. Wicked foreigners who had settled on the isle told the natives that the missionaries had introduced and were spreading the disease. Hostilities arose among the tribes — robberies and murders; Mr Sturges's house was burnt, and he and his family driven into the woods.

Still the mission-party toiled in hope. In four years' time they had printed portions of the Scriptures and hymns in Ponapean, and assembling the people in schools, persuaded them to learn. After eight years had elapsed, they had the joy of receiving three converts as members of the Church— shortly followed by eight more. Persecution ensued, with the usual result of an increase of converts. At length a little chapel was built in the mountains; others followed. The king, after long vibrating between good and evil, now professed himself a Christian. In 1867, religious services were held regularly at twelve principal places; the church numbered 160 communicants, the schools 1000 readers, and many others were waiting to be admitted to baptism. So the work progressed.

Meanwhile the Hawaiian Mission extended its operations to other groups. In 1857, a vessel had been sent from America for this especial service. She was called the Morning Star, and was emphatically "the children's ship," built by the contributions of the New England Sunday-schools. She brought Mr and Mrs Bingham (son of the Hawaiian pioneer), and Kanakaole and his wife. Dr Pierson and Mr Doane and their wives had preceded them, each accompanied by Hawaiian teachers. Their object was to establish missions on the sixteen isles which compose the Gilbert or Kingsmill group, and the thirty Marshall Isles—Apaiang being the spot apparently most favourable in the former group, and Ebon in the latter.

These offered no sort of natural attraction, being miserable low coral-isles, scarcely raised above the water-level. The Gilbert Isles lie actually on the equator, which implies a climate almost unendurable to a white man, though less trying to the native teacher. One language is spoken throughout the group, by a population of about 40,000 persons, and it is marked by a prevalence of vowelled syllables, greatly resembling that of Hawaii. From this circumstance it appeared to be a field in which the Hawaiian teachers would work at a considerable advantage.

But there were many hardships to face, chiefly from the scarcity of food. The only vegetable cultivated is a very inferior kind of *kalo* (or *taro*), and the staple of life is the cocoa-nut, eked out with a coarse flour like sawdust, prepared from the woody fruit of the *pandanus* or screw-pine. Fish is to be had, but there is no wood for fuel, so it must be eaten raw, which, however, is not accounted a great hardship. Of course the cocoa-palm furnishes meat and drink; but it makes a dull meal, even when its unwilling sap has been tormented into yielding molasses and rum. In these isles it furnishes the only timber for house-building, while its leaves supply thatch, and also clothing, mats, and cords.

A very narrow girdle for men, and a mat for women, is the approved dress, which is supplemented by very elaborate tattooing. The people are polygamists, and their religion is a vague spirit-worship, without priest, idol, or temple.

Such are the isles where Mr and Mrs Bingham settled, with several Hawaiian assistants. They have toiled for many years, and still account it to be but seed-time. Up to the year 1870, they could only count fifty hopeful converts.

But much preparatory work has been done at the Apaiang printing-press, where all the translations made for the use of this Micronesian Mission are sent to be printed. Up to the same date this printing-press had issued for Ponape 381,600 pages; for Kusaie, 223,200; for the Marshall Isles, 381,726; and for the Gilbert Isles, 1,050,192.

The Marshall Isles lie to the north-west of the

Gilbert Isles. They are of the same low coral-formation, but are more fertile, and produce breadfruit and bananas. At the time when the Mission was commenced, the population was estimated at 12,000, speaking different dialects, very unlike Hawaiian. The people bore a character for extreme ferocity, which caused these isles to be shunned by foreign vessels. This, to the missionaries, was a strong point of advantage in beginning work, though the alleged ferocity was a drawback. The latter was most strangely and providentially overcome.

As the Morning Star set sail for this group, the party were warned by old sea-captains of the dangers they were about to incur; and as they neared Ebon Isle, the captain put up his boarding-nettings, stationed his men fore and aft, and anxiously awaited the issue. Fifteen canoes came out to meet the vessel, all crowded with men. In the prow of the foremost stood a powerful savage, with huge rings in his ears, and his head wreathed with flowers. As the canoes drew near, Dr Pierson called to the people in their own language, and in another moment he and the leader recognised one another as old friends, and the savage sprang on board shouting, "Doctor! Doctor!" in ecstatic delight. The news flew along the canoes, and the joyous shout was re-echoed by all.

Then the wondering captain learnt that in the

previous year five canoes, having ninety men on board, had been driven by a tempest from the Marshall Isles, and after fifteen days at sea, at last reached Kusaie, where, according to the laws of savages, small hospitality would have awaited them had not the missionaries rescued them, given them food and medicine, and shown them great kindness.

Then, when the favouring monsoon set in, they returned in safety to their own homes, where now they, in their turn, welcomed the mission-party; and when these returned a few days later to disembark, they were received by crowds, shouting, singing, and dancing for joy; and the king's sister, a venerable chiefess, came out, and, taking Dr Pierson by both hands, led him to her house with all possible honour. Thus was the way made smooth for beginning the mission-work among a race of reputed cannibals.

Though progress has not been very rapid, it has been steady; and in 1870 the church of the Marshall Isles numbered a hundred and forty communicants, which, of course, implies a very large number of church attendants. A large share of this success is due to the devoted labours of the Hawaiian teachers, ten of whom are now working in Micronesia as ordained ministers.

But the field which they have especially made their own is that of the Marquesas Isles, from which, in 1797, the London Mission were so quickly driven by the exceeding fierceness of the cannibal inhabitants, and where the American Mission proved equally unsuccessful in 1833.[1]

But in 1853, a Marquesan chief came to the Sandwich Isles, and requested that teachers should be sent to his people. Mr Bickrell, an English layman, agreed to return with him, accompanied by four Hawaiian teachers and their wives. The names of these brave volunteers were the Rev. James Kekela (the first ordained of the native pastors), who had already commenced the Hawaiian Mission in Micronesia, and the Rev. Samuel Kauwealoha, with Lot Kauaihelani and Isaia Kaiwi, deacons.

The Rev. Mr Parker, of the American Mission, accompanied this little band, to advise and help them in beginning their work; and the great stone church in Honolulu was crowded with an earnest congregation of those who, having themselves so recently found the Great Light, were now so anxious to dispense it to the lands still sunk in degrading darkness.

The experiment proved successful. It was found that the jealous policy of France, which made the position of foreign missionaries untenable, was less inimical to the Hawaiian teachers: so, notwith-

[1] See 'A Lady's Cruise in a French Man-of-War' (C. F. Gordon Cumming), vol. ii. pp. 106-125.

standing the opposition of the Roman Catholic priests, who endeavoured to have them sent away, their number was shortly increased, and in 1864 there were eighteen male and female Hawaiian teachers settled in the Marquesas; and so bravely did they stand by their colours (enduring all manner of hardships and trials, at the hands of white men and brown), that they succeeded in making many converts.

Grievous to say, however, from one cause or another, chiefly from the very rapid depopulation of Hawaii, it has been found impossible to keep up the supply of teachers both in the Marquesas and in Micronesia, so the former has of late been sadly neglected. Out of the ten mission-stations which had been successfully established in different parts of the group, seven have, most reluctantly, been abandoned, as there are at present only three teachers remaining. Happily, a large number of the Marquesan converts (so recently barbarous savages) have learnt to read for themselves " the old, old story," taught them by these Hawaiian apostles, and so the lessons of these brave men will not be forgotten; and it is hoped that ere long the London Mission may send teachers from Tahiti to take up the work so well begun.

The Tahitians, being now French subjects, would have the advantage of claiming civil rights, which would place them on a par with the members of the Roman Catholic Mission. These have been working in the Marquesas for upwards of forty years, but have as yet failed even to civilise the people—such progress as has been made being clearly traceable to the influence of the Hawaiian teachers.

So Hawaii has earned a good right to rank as a successful missionary church; and popular interest in the subject is so well maintained, that every parish throughout Hawaii-nei pays an annual contribution to the Foreign Mission Society of the little island kingdom.

She has even done her part in helping to carry the Light to Japan. And when King Kalakaua recently visited that wonderful land, none welcomed him more cordially than the members of "the Native Church of Christ in Japan," who reminded him that his own subjects had contributed liberally to the building and organisation of their church. Thus this Christian infant has helped to found the new building which, ere long, will assuredly arise on the ruins of the once stately but now fast decaying systems of that grand ancient civilisation.

The parent Society having, in 1863, decided that the church in Hawaii was sufficiently well established to become national and self-governing, commenced the work of training the native ministers for their new and very responsible position.

It was decided that all church business should be organised by a "Hawaiian Evangelical Association," which should conduct all its deliberations in the Hawaiian tongue, and at which native pastors and delegates were to take their place on equal terms with the American missionaries.

The result was found to answer beyond their expectations. About five years later, some of the fathers of the Mission, who had been least hopeful of the success of this measure, acknowledged themselves thoroughly satisfied. In their report they speak of the sixty Hawaiian members who constitute the bulk of the assembly, as an earnest body of men, generally rather cautious, but ever ready to fall in with progressive ideas. "For the first time we elected a Hawaiian as moderator. He is a good man, and he did well."

Yet it is open to question whether it would not have been wiser to have retained a larger number of foreign pastors. Some of those most competent to judge, consider that, though the movement seemed to answer admirably at first, while the native pastors were men whose habit it was to refer to their white teachers in every difficult question, the present generation, who have no such counsellors at hand (and who, in any case, believe themselves to be quite as wise as their teachers), are very apt to fail in judgment; and so church discipline has become slack, and zeal has become more rare.

Though modelled on the Congregational system, no sectarian name is tolerated. The Hawaiians wish to be known simply as Christians. The group is now divided into 56 "Church organisations," with 120 churches. Of these, only five are in charge of Americans. All the others are in the hands of native pastors, many of whom are acknowledged, even by foreigners, to be men of decided ability and real eloquence.

Such facts speak for themselves. Nevertheless, it is not to be supposed that the work of even sixty years could have effectually rooted out all elements of evil from any race, far less from a people of the Hawaiian temperament, and so constantly surrounded by adverse influences. But a vast deal has already been accomplished, and steady progress has been made.

A most important movement was the establishment of more boarding-schools for girls. Though the supply was not equal to the need, several had been continuing their work steadily for many years. Miss Ogden's girls' school was commenced in 1828, and continued for nearly forty years, during which hundreds of girls were carefully trained by her. On Maui, on Kauai, in Honolulu, and in various parts of the group, upwards of a dozen American ladies had established boarding-schools for from twenty to thirty girls each.

I particularise these, because it has been somewhat unfairly stated by unfriendly pens that the work of training girls had been shamefully neglected, and that the amount of immorality which prevails, after sixty years of Christian teaching, speaks little for the method adopted by the American Mission.

I wonder whether those writers ever studied the statistics of their own British Isles, after thirteen hundred years of highly approved Christian teaching.[1]

[1] St Columba landed in Scotland A.D. 563. In this nineteenth century the statistics for the principal towns in Scotland give very nearly one-tenth of the births as illegitimate. In certain counties the proportion is very much higher,—in Wigtown, 17; in Elgin, 16; Banff and Aberdeen, 15 and 14 per cent. Lest this statement should be deemed incredible, I subjoin the return for the counties of Scotland in the year 1880:—

PROPORTION OF ILLEGITIMATE TO EVERY 100 BIRTHS IN SCOTLAND, ITS DIVISIONS AND COUNTIES, IN 1880.

Divisions.	Per cent of Illegit.	Counties.	Per cent of Illegit.	Counties.	Per cent of Illegit.
Scotland,	8.4	Caithness,	11.4	Argyll,	7.7
		Sutherland,	5.3	Bute,	6.4
Northern Division,	7.7	Ross & Cromarty,	4.8	Renfrew,	6.1
North-Western Do.	6.7	Inverness,	7.9	Ayr,	7.9
North-Eastern Do.	14.6	Nairn,	10.0	Lanark,	6.7
East-Midland Do.	8.9	Elgin,	16.8	Linlithgow,	7.3
West-Midland Do.	6.4	Banff,	15.8	Edinburgh,	7.3
South-Western Do.	6.8	Aberdeen,	14.4	Haddington,	6.0
South-Eastern Do.	7.5	Kincardine,	12.1	Berwick,	9.9
Southern Do.	14.2	Forfar,	9.9	Peebles,	10.3
		Perth,	9.2	Selkirk,	8.6
		Fife,	6.8	Roxburgh,	11.0
Counties.		Kinross,	10.3	Dumfries,	13.8
		Clackmannan,	8.2	Kirkcudbright,	15.9
Shetland,	5.5	Stirling,	6.8	Wigtown,	17.9
Orkney,	5.6	Dumbarton,	4.8		

Ireland, though superior in this respect, yet, after a still longer period of Christian teaching, supplies us almost daily with such incidents of treacherous brutality as were rarely equalled, never surpassed, by the heathen islanders of the Pacific.

By the way, while touching on this unpleasant topic, I may remark that if it were possible for the law to enforce strict morality, Hawaii ought to be a pattern kingdom.

A case occurred just before my arrival which was of deep interest to "society" in Honolulu. Its details were so generally known, that I may venture to repeat them, as they were told to me by one intimately acquainted with all the persons concerned, and well versed in Hawaiian law.

One of the most respected residents in Honolulu is a wealthy Chinaman. He holds a high place in society; his sons are distinguishing themselves in American colleges, and his large family of daughters are said to be very well-educated and attractive girls.

The eldest was wooed and won by a young Englishman, who was well known and much liked in the community. The father was pleased: he heaped wealth on the young couple, furnished and gave them a house; and the gay wedding was honoured by the presence of the king and queen, and of all the *élite* of Honolulu.

Not many days afterwards, news came from a remote country district that a white girl, living in her parents' home, had given birth to a child, of which she declared the bridegroom to be the father. He was arrested, and tried on the simplest charge of immorality. There was not a suggestion of any promise of marriage, or any complicating circumstances. By the plain law as it stands, Mr G. had to pay a fine of $5000 (£1000), in addition to three months of hard labour in prison dress, breaking stones in the streets of Honolulu.

When his term of imprisonment had expired, he determined to leave the island. His father-in-law brought some further action; and finally, the young man contrived to escape in a rowing-boat, and reached a sailing-ship, which conveyed him to China.

In this instance public interest was accentuated by the fact that the mother of the child was a foreigner, immorality amongst white girls being almost unknown.

I heard of another instance in which the law had been somewhat severely carried out. The sister of the late king is supposed to have been somewhat too intimate in her relations with various of her own countrymen. These little irregularities were allowed to pass unnoticed; but finally, she was detected in an intrigue with a white man, who thereupon was banished from the kingdom of Hawaii, his wife and children not being allowed to accompany him.

With regard to the disparaging comments that have been so freely showered on the Christian work done in Hawaii, because of the immorality which still prevails, I cannot do better than quote the following words of Dr Gulick, than whom none has had better opportunity of forming a true estimate of progress. He says:—

"The number of virtuous men and women has been steadily increasing from the beginning of the mission-work. The breakwater against the terrible ocean of licence has been laid deep and permanent. It has in many places so nearly reached the surface, that female virtue is now a known fact on these sunny isles, where, a few years ago, the name was unknown, and the fact unheard of. A public sentiment on this subject is gradually being created, in spite of terrible counter-influences.

"But for the preserving control of the Gospel during the last half-century, there would have been now scarcely a Hawaiian left to tell the story of the extinction of the race through foreign vices, grafted upon natural depravity. That the race still continues to decrease is no wonder. That there is still so much vice and immorality should astonish no one. But that the race still exists, and that there is any virtue, any piety, any civilisation, is a matter for deepest thankfulness."

And, humanly speaking, the good that has been done in Hawaii-nei has undoubtedly been due to the labours of the American Congregational Mission.

CHAPTER XXI.

ESTABLISHMENT OF THE ROMAN CATHOLIC MISSION—THE LAPLACE TREATY—UNJUST CLAIMS BY FRENCH AND ENGLISH SHIPS—DECLARATION OF INDEPENDENCE—THE REFORMED CATHOLIC MISSION—DEATH OF THE PRINCE OF HAWAII AND OF KAMEHAMEHA IV.

THERE is no chapter in the story of missions so painful as that which, in almost every instance of good work done, records the conflicts of Christian sects, when the servants of one Master (each seeking to do His will according to their lights, yet unable to co-operate) bring discord in lieu of harmony, and each hinders the growth of the good seed planted by his neighbour—at least for so long as the plants are young and tender. Of course, when each has made a position for itself, they flourish side by side, as in older communities.

The three regiments of "the grand army" which have found their way to Hawaii are—first, as we have seen, the American Congregational Mission, established A.D. 1820.

Secondly, the Roman Catholic, which commenced a struggling existence in 1827.

Thirdly, the English Episcopal, which, under the title of the Reformed Catholic Church, commenced its work in 1862.

The Roman Mission was commenced on a very small scale. A French Jesuit priest, with an Irish assistant and four mechanics, was landed at Honolulu by a French ship, with little baggage save church ornaments. The captain was informed by the governor of the law forbidding any person to land without obtaining the king's permission. This, however, he ignored, and forthwith sailed, leaving the priests to make the best arrangement they could.

In this dilemma the chiefs showed them kindness, but with one accord agreed that they should not be allowed to settle on the isles. The principal spokesman in the matter was Boki, a high chief, who had accompanied his royal master to England, and had himself been honoured by an interview with George IV. at Windsor. Having acquired some knowledge of the distinctions between the Roman and Protestant creeds (though little sympathy with either), he very wisely surmised that to allow teachers of both to establish themselves in so small a country would create unpleasant dissensions, and as the chiefs were already favourably inclined to the American teachers, they decided to admit no others. They stated plainly that, had the French priests arrived first, they should have been allowed to possess the field, but that two sets of teachers were not required.

Nevertheless, as these strangers had no means of immediate departure, no objection was offered to their opening a small chapel for their own worship, and that of a few foreigners. Curiosity attracted some natives to witness the ceremonies, and they speedily reported that images were worshipped. This created so much surprise, that many chiefs, including the young king (Kamehameha III.), went to judge and inquire for themselves, when they were simultaneously struck with the analogies to the system they had abandoned, in the use of images, the rigid fasts, and the veneration of relics. They declared that "this new religion is all about worshipping images, and dead men's bones, and *tabus* on meat." So they decided emphatically that nothing of the sort should be tolerated.

The priests, however, maintained their ground quietly. By the courtesy of the American missionaries, they were furnished with copies of their works in the Hawaiian tongue, to enable them to prosecute their studies, and slowly but surely the work of proselytism was commenced.

There were still some among the people who

in their hearts clung to their old worship, and would fain have cherished their idols as outward visible symbols of the spiritual beings whom they had reverenced in the past. These were greatly attracted by the pictures and images in the chapel. Others were easily won by teaching which neither forbade the use of stimulants, nor the dances and revels, which the Americans denounced. So, ere long, a small number declared themselves in favour of the prohibited worship.

The chiefs had been too long accustomed to implicit obedience, to understand liberty of conscience; so these disobedient subjects were called to account and punished. The American missionaries, though naturally not sympathetic towards the new-comers, felt bound to remonstrate against this action, and pointed out to the chiefs that the offenders had infringed no law. Whereupon the Regent Kaahamanu referred him to the Hawaiian edict against idolatry, promulgated in 1819, and pointed out wherein the new worship resembled that which they had abandoned of their own accord.

Besides which, it was the will of the chiefs, that the Decalogue should be the foundation of Hawaiian law; and was it not therein written, "Thou shalt not *bow down* before a graven image"? So the converts to the new faith were subjected to imprisonment and compulsory work, until

American love of fair-play induced the chiefs to establish a law of liberty in matters of conscience.

As a matter of course, the opposition of the chiefs was attributed by the priests to the influence of the Protestant missionaries; whereas, to all who remembered the iconoclastic outburst which accompanied the spontaneous overthrow of image-worship in Hawaii, it was a perfectly natural sequence.

Many of the foreign residents, however, contrived to make it a party question, and various malcontents were induced to join them; so the numbers increased, and a considerable faction hostile to the Government was formed. Then the high chiefs deemed it necessary to act with decision, and ordered the priests to leave the isles within three months.

As no notice whatever was taken of this command, the Government decided that it was necessary that they should be sent away at the public expense; so a brig was chartered, at the cost of a thousand dollars, to convey them to California, where the Prefect of the Roman Mission had invited them to aid him in his work among the Indians.

In the following year an Irish priest landed, and a few months later, the banished priests returned from California. The chiefs, of course, refused to allow them to remain; but two out of the three being Irishmen, the English consul claimed their right so to do. The chiefs insisted on re-shipping the offenders; but ere the vessel left the port, an English man-of-war, and a French frigate commanded by Admiral Du Petit Thouars, arrived.

At the request of Mr Charlton and the priests, the latter were forcibly rescued and brought ashore, escorted by the two commanders and a body of marines. The princess-regent, Kinau (who, on the death of Queen Kaahumanu, had succeeded to her office as Kuhina-nui, which was practically that of Prime Minister), urged the English captain to investigate matters himself, but he replied that he must accept the statements of the consul. The latter "bullied and stormed, and finally shook his fist in Kinau's face."[1] Eventually, however, it was conceded that the king had the right to exclude whomsoever he pleased from his dominions, and that the priests must go.

A treaty of peace and amity between France and the Sandwich Isles was then signed.

In 1839, the French sixty-gun frigate Artemise, commanded by Captain Laplace, arrived off Honolulu, and sent ashore a most startling manifesto, addressed to the king in the name of the king of France, declaring that the insults which he had

[1] Jarves's History of Hawaii. Published 1844.

dared to offer to France in the person of her priests must be atoned for—that perfect freedom must be accorded to the exercise of the Catholic religion throughout the isles—that a site for a Catholic church must be given at Honolulu—and that a sum of 20,000 dollars must be deposited in the hands of the captain of the Artemise, as a pledge for the fulfilment of these conditions.

This document was accompanied by letters to the foreign consuls, to state that, as, in the event of non-compliance, he would be compelled to bombard the town, he offered an asylum on board the frigate to all foreigners, except such as were in any way connected with the Protestant Mission.

Great alarm naturally spread among the people. The French were reported to have openly declared, that if fighting commenced, they would carry fire and sword through the isles. The king was absent, on the isle of Maui. The good princess-regent, Kinau, had recently died, and she had been succeeded in office by her sister Kekauluohi, who was her inferior in decision and strength of intellect. A final answer was required within five days; and as the king had not returned, the treaty was signed by the princess-regent and the governor. The 20,000 dols. were borrowed with great difficulty, and at high interest, from foreign merchants, and were carried on board. The tricoloured flag received the stipulated salute, which was promptly returned.

The French commander then came ashore, escorted by 200 seamen with fixed bayonets, and the band of the frigate, to celebrate a military Mass. The place selected for the ceremony was a large native house belonging to the king, who arrived in time to witness this high-handed proceeding.

Having successfully carried this point, M. Laplace was further induced to employ the persuasive influence of his Big Guns, in obtaining a treaty, containing a clause legalising the import of all French merchandise, *with special reference to wines and brandy*, at a duty not to exceed five per cent.

The king had, by the advice of his council, prohibited the introduction of all ardent spirits into his kingdom, and laid a heavy duty on wines. The result had been so excellent, in the improved condition of the ports, that the majority of the foreign residents were in favour of this measure. The French consul, however, boasted of his determination to have his liquor free, or nearly so; and, at his request, the treaty with this obnoxious clause was drawn up and sent to the king one evening, requiring him to sign it by breakfast-time on the following morning, without option of amendment or alteration.

Rumours were circulated, so as to reach the king's ears, that, should he refuse, there would be no end of trouble, and that ultimately a strong force would come and take possession of his isles. With sore reluctance, not knowing what might follow, he signed the treaty—at the same time making ineffectual protests against the wrong done to himself and to his country by this compulsory mode of action,—might against right.

The French consul lost no time in profiting by the extorted privilege. Very soon his own ship arrived from Valparaiso with a cargo of liquors.

The evils resulting from the unlimited supply of brandy soon became so alarming, that the Government endeavoured, by imposing a system of licences, to restrain the internal traffic, which was inundating every part of the group with fire-water. The French consul construed this into a violation of the treaty, on the ground that any restriction implied an equal one on importation.

Consequently, the next French man-of-war which arrived (in 1842), was by him induced to make vehement remonstrance on the subject, accompanied by a long list of grievances and demands, with the usual shadowy suggestions of impending evil should they be refused.

Happily, on this occasion the king was able to return a manly and dignified answer, maintaining his own rights, and stating that he had already despatched ministers to Louis Philippe to negotiate a new treaty. This silenced the French commander, who, however, sailed without according the customary salute.

Just at this time, the king also deemed it necessary to send special commissioners to England, to represent various matters. The English consul—who, ever since his appointment in 1825, had acted a most unfriendly part both to the native Government and to the American Mission—now behaved so recklessly, in his determination to keep up the fiction that the islanders were subjects of Great Britain, that the king determined to demand from each Great Power an acknowledgment of the independence of the isles, and a guarantee against their usurpation by any country.

Happily, Sir George Simpson, and Dr M'Laughlin of the Hudson Bay Company, happened to arrive on a visit to the isles, and were so strongly impressed with the injustice done to the native Government by some of their countrymen, that Sir George undertook the office of commissioner for the king, and at once sailed for London, whither he was speedily followed by Mr Charlton, who, ere he embarked, despatched to the king a letter so insulting, that on its being reported to the Home Government, it resulted in his dismissal from office.

Ere he departed, he appointed a vice-consul, whom the king refused to receive, but who insisted on retaining the office.

On his way to England, Mr Charlton fell in with Lord George Paulet, commanding H.B.M. frigate Carysfort, on his way to Honolulu, and so influenced him, that, on arriving at that port, the customary salutes were withheld; and an interview with the vice-consul led to such measures, on the part of Lord George, as resulted (25th February 1843) in a provisional cession of the isles to Great Britain, though under protest against the extreme injustice of the proceeding, and an appeal to England for redress.

For the next five months all insular affairs were in a deplorable state, and the condition of Honolulu reminded the early settlers of the palmy days of heathenism. The king, finding himself powerless, retired to the isle of Maui. The chiefs had no option but to await, in longing hope, the justice which they confidently expected from England. But in the meanwhile, no laws could be enforced: all barriers to drunkenness and immorality were set aside, while to the population of a harbour already crowded with shipping, were added the sailors of two men-of-war; and these were shortly followed by two large frigates, with 1200 men—an influx not conducive to order and quiet!

This painful state of matters continued till the beginning of July, when the American commodore (Kearney) arrived, and immediately issued a public protest against the seizure of the isles, and treated the chiefs as independent princes. The king returned from Maui to hold conference with the commodore, whose courtesy to the native monarch so exasperated Lord George, that further trouble appeared imminent, when, on the 26th July, Rear-Admiral Thomas arrived unexpectedly from Valparaiso, whence he had hurried in hot haste on receiving Lord George's despatches.

By every means in his power he sought to atone for the indignity that had been done to the king and people; and the former, on the 31st July, was reinstated in his authority in the most formal and honourable manner. Immediately after this ceremony, the king and chiefs repaired to the Kawaiahao, or great stone church, to return thanks for this timely interposition of Providence.

From that time forward, the 31st of July has been celebrated as a national day of thanksgiving and rejoicing for the restoration of the national independence. It is to Hawaii-nei what the 4th of July is to the United States.

The memory of Admiral Thomas is still held in grateful honour throughout the isles.

In 1843, a special commissioner was sent to the

isles to represent the United States, and in the following year a consul-general was sent by Great Britain.

In May 1845, the king, for the first time, opened the Legislative Chamber in person, and business was transacted in the most ceremonious manner.

In 1846, the king of France sent a special commissioner, bearing a treaty concerted between France and England, in which all the objectionable clauses inserted in previous negotiations were so modified as to be more tolerable, and the 20,000 dollars exacted by Captain Laplace were returned.

In the same year came a Danish man-of-war, to negotiate a treaty on behalf of the king of Denmark—memorable as being the first occasion on which a foreign Power fully recognised the sovereign rights of the king of Hawaii.

Three years elapsed, when once again the Big Guns of France were brought to bear on poor peaceful Honolulu.

The Marquesas had been quietly annexed. The Society Isles had been taken "under protection" by France. It can only be supposed that she was craving to extend her care over Hawaii also. Be that as it may, in 1849 Rear-Admiral Tromelin arrived in a heavily armed frigate, presented certain wholly unreasonable and unjust demands, and, on their being refused, took military possession of the fort, the Government offices, the custom-house, the king's yacht, and all vessels sailing under the Hawaiian flag. The fort was dismantled, the arms and powder destroyed, and the yacht sent off to Tahiti.

Taught by past experience, the Government offered no resistance, but the representatives of the United States and Great Britain made a formal protest. The admiral did not deem it prudent to press his demands. Neither did he restore the king's yacht.

Yet one more offensive effort was made by France. In 1850, M. Perrin was sent out in a French man-of-war as commissioner of the republic, prepared to enforce the demands made by Admiral Tromelin. Happily, just at the critical moment of the negotiations, the United States ship Vandalia came into port, and her presence had the effect of inducing the French commissioner to waive his most offensive demands.

Thenceforward no further molestation was offered.

Meanwhile very great damage had been done by the flood of cheap liquor that had been introduced since the Laplace treaty. In too many instances the old thirst for ardent spirits was reawakened, and it was evident to the king and chiefs that strong efforts must be made to counteract the evil. Many of them had themselves been hard drinkers in past years, so they fully realised the temptation thus forced upon their people.

Being unable to check its importation, they could only strive, by influence and example, to create a public feeling on the subject. For this reason, the king and most of the chiefs pledged themselves to total abstinence, and became zealous preachers of temperance, the king himself frequently addressing the people on the subject, and with such good effect, that temperance societies were formed all over the isles, and proved of the greatest benefit. Thousands of children also enlisted in "the cold-water army," and formed a powerful band of hope.

In 1840, the king, with the concurrence of the chiefs, had taken a very remarkable step for what he considered to be the welfare of his people— namely, that, of his own free will, he granted a sort of *Magna Charta* of Hawaiian rights, voluntarily sweeping away all the old feudal privileges, which for generations had given absolute power to the chiefs, and to himself over all. He now bestowed on his subjects full constitutional freedom, with a written code of most just laws, granting to his people the free enjoyment of all rights of property, with full liberty of conscience and of action. The laws regulated the rent of lands, the descent of property, the poll-tax, the fisheries, and all other matters of importance. Previous to this, the people had no well-defined rights. They might at any moment be ejected from their homes at the will of the chiefs, who might also appropriate all the produce of their fields or of their fishing, and compel them to work unpaid for their feudal lords.

In drawing up the charter, the king was assisted by Mr Richards, who, at the request of the chiefs, had relinquished his connection with the Mission, that he might assume the duties of counsellor and teacher of political economy.

This was a very noteworthy instance of a hereditary despotic Government voluntarily curtailing its own power for what appeared to be the good of the people, and is the more remarkable as being the deliberate act of men who, twenty years previously, had taken their first great stride towards liberty in the abolition of the *tabu*, while they were still heathens and savages of the most unmitigated class.

One of the provisions in the new code was to the effect that parents having four children living with them should be freed from all labour for the chiefs; and if there were five children, the parents should be exempt from all taxation. Afterwards it was enacted that families having three children should be free from taxation, and those with a larger number should receive gifts of land and other encouragements to industry. This was a premium on the increase of the population, which points to the painful anxiety caused by the grievous depopulation of the group. Formerly, every head was taxed,—a fruitful source of infanticide, as each child became an additional burden.

Ever since the isles have been known, this distressing fact has been only too apparent, and every census taken in Hawaii-nei proves that the race is swiftly and surely fading from the earth.

By Captain Cook's estimate, made just a century ago, the population of the isles was reckoned at 400,000. It was long supposed that this was utterly erroneous, being based on the crowds assembled to see the strangers. It was also supposed that early travellers, who spoke of the traces of old villages and lands once cultivated, but then abandoned, made no allowance for the nomadic habits of the people. But later experience has gone to support the probability that the original computation may, after all, not have been greatly in excess. Everything goes to show that depopulation was never so rapid as in the reigns of the great Kamehameha and his successor—that is to say, the forty years after Cook's visit.

The first missionaries, arriving in 1820, estimated the population of the group at 140,000. But even then, the Hawaiians themselves assured them that the population had diminished three-fourths within the previous forty years, owing to their sanguinary inter-insular wars, the increase of infanticide, and of numerous diseases.

In 1832, it was reckoned at 130,000. In 1836, it was 108,000. The census taken in 1850 gives 84,000, and in that year the number of deaths was proved to be 2900 in excess of the births.

In 1867-68-69, the decrease was regular—a thousand per annum. In 1872, the total number of natives was 49,044, and of half-castes, 2487.

In 1878, the census of the whole group was as follows:—

Natives,	44,088
Half-castes,	3,420
Chinese,	5,916
Americans,	1,276
Britons,	883
Portuguese,	436
Germans,	272
French,	81
Other foreigners,	666
Foreign children born in the isles,	947

While the pure Hawaiian blood is thus grievously fading from the earth, it is happily found that the mixed race possesses considerable vitality, and is steadily increasing. The statistics of the Board of Education show that thirteen per cent of the children attending the Government schools are half-caste, seventy-nine per cent are purely Hawaiian, and the rest are foreigners.

Nevertheless, it is evident that, unless some

almost miraculous change occurs speedily, the pure race of Hawaii must become extinct within half a century.

It is curious to observe how closely the same process of fading away, "like snowdrift in thaw," has befallen the kindred race of Maoris in New Zealand, who are supposed to have come originally from Hawaii. In A.D. 1861, their total number was found to have dwindled to 55,000. In 1879, it had still further diminished to 43,000.

It is also worthy of note that in both countries the indigenous plants and birds seem to be giving way to imported ones. As to animals, scarcely any existed in either land; but such as there were, speedily disappeared.

In the year 1852, the king was induced to follow up the "Bill of Rights," by agreeing to universal suffrage, vote by ballot, paid members, and no property qualification, — in short, a complete democracy.

Eight years later, Kamehameha V. concluded that this concession had been unwise, and so the constitution was remodelled. Thenceforth no man was entitled to a vote who had not either an income of at least £15 a-year, or real estate to the value of £30. The House of Representatives was to consist of forty members, possessing real estate to the value of £100, or an income of £50; the Privy

Council to consist of thirty members, and a Cabinet Council.

During the years which had elapsed since the Laplace treaty, the Romish priests had not been idle. A bishop, bearing the title of Arathea,[1] had been appointed to take charge of the mission, aided by a vicar-apostolic and a party of " sisters." The French branch of the Propaganda at Lyons had kept them amply supplied with funds for all purposes. Thus they had been enabled to build a cathedral at Honolulu, and stone churches at all the principal places in the isles, and had succeeded in gathering a considerable number of adherents.

As a matter of course, the ever-grievous war of sectarianism had raged, as it had become necessary for the Protestant teachers to bring points of difference prominently forward.

But they, too, had continued to work earnestly, and were satisfied that the general tone of the people was one of continual progress, with an occasional stride. Thus, in 1860, a great revival-wave seemed to pass over the isles—a period of extraordinary earnestness, which resulted in an addition of upwards of two thousand to the previous number of communicants.

[1] When the Church of Rome creates a new bishopric in heathen lands, *in partibus infidelium*, it bestows on it the title of some extinct diocese of the ancient Church.

Happily, as years have rolled on, all the early antagonisms have died out, and these two great branches of the Christian army have learnt to work side by side in peace. As I write these words, tidings reach me of the death of Bishop Maigret (on June 12, 1882); and I read, in the most Protestant paper of Honolulu, an expression of the deep regret experienced throughout the isles at the death of the venerable and universally respected prelate of the Catholic Church on the Hawaiian islands, with comments on his long and useful career, since he landed in the isles in 1837.

The writer goes on to speak of the high esteem in which, not only his co-religionists, but the community at large, hold "the useful and laborious Father Hermann," who is appointed successor to Bishop Maigret.

So truly does time mellow all things.

To return from the present day to matters of recent history.

Kamehameha III. died in December 1854. His memory is cherished throughout Hawaii-nei as that of the good and just sovereign who voluntarily bestowed on his people their charter of liberty, and ever strove to act for their welfare.

Having married a woman of inferior rank, her children were not eligible for the throne. He therefore nominated as his successor his nephew, Liho

Liho Iolani (third son of the late princess-regent, Kinau, and of the high chief Kekuanoa), who consequently was now proclaimed king, under the title of Kamehameha IV.

Soon after his accession, he married Kaleleonalani (commonly called Emma), the adopted daughter of Dr Rooke, and granddaughter of John Young,[1] whose marriage with a high chiefess had, according to Hawaiian custom, bequeathed noble birth to his descendants. Young left two daughters, one of whom married Dr Rooke, and died without issue. The other sister, Fanny Young, married a Hawaiian, and was the mother of Queen Emma.

The young king was naturally of a refined and highly sensitive nature. He had received a sound English education, and had, further, the advantage of having travelled considerably. He spoke and wrote English perfectly, and keenly enjoyed such authors as Longfellow and Tennyson, or Charles Kingsley.

From his early youth he had been beloved by the Hawaiians, on account of his ever-ready sympathy and kindness to the humblest. When, in 1853, the terrible scourge of smallpox raged in the isles, he had been foremost in caring for the sick, entering the plague-stricken huts, that he might himself minister to their necessities.

[1] See chap. xvi.

And afterwards, he and Queen Emma devoted their energies to erecting the admirable hospital which forms his abiding monument. In order to raise the necessary funds, the king himself visited every house and shop in Honolulu, note-book in hand, with a genial smile and a pleasant word for every one, seeming personally grateful to each subscriber who helped on the good work. Thus he himself collected 6000 dollars, which enabled him to carry out his heart's desire, in building a comfortable, airy hospital, with ample accommodation for a hundred patients—men's wards on the ground-floor, and women above. Many a poor sufferer has there been soothed and cheered by the gentle sympathy of the king or queen.

Now "The Queen's Hospital" is the first thing that presents itself to the notice of all new-comers, as it is supported by a tax of two dollars, payable by every person landing on the isles. And the visitor whose interest prompts him to visit the hospital, is welcomed to a bright, pleasant house, with constantly renewed flowers to cheer the patients.

The year 1862 was marked by the commencement of an Episcopal Mission, which, whatever may be its ultimate advantages, certainly did not, in the first instance, tend to the growth of those fruits of righteousness which are "sown in peace," inasmuch as its primary result was a stirring up of most painful religious discussions, and of such grievously bitter party spirit, as most effectually brushes the down from the delicate and sensitive wings of devotion.

The chief promoter of the movement was Mr Wyllie, a Scotchman, and a zealous Episcopalian, who arrived in the isles in 1845, and held office as Foreign Minister for nearly a quarter of a century. Being naturally desirous for the services of his own Church, he applied repeatedly to the Bishop of California,[1] requesting that an Episcopal clergyman might be sent to Honolulu. Having none who could be spared, the bishop applied to the Foreign Committee in New York, who, however, replied that, "not considering the Sandwich Isles a heathen land, it was not within their field."

During the young king's visit to England, in 1847, he and his brother had attended the service in Westminster Abbey, where the solemnity of the beautiful music, and the grandeur of the glorious building, had deeply impressed them both. The king, therefore, lent a willing ear to Mr Wyllie's urgent desire that he should apply to England for a chaplain, who should also undertake the early education of the little Crown-prince. The suggestion also found favour with Queen Emma, who had

[1] William Ingraham Kip, Bishop of California.

been partly educated by an English lady, and, by her, trained according to the principles of the English Church, of which her adopted father, Dr Rooke, was a member.

It so happened that the Bishops of California and of New York were both in England at the time when this request was received. The matter was fully discussed by them with the Bishops of Oxford and London; and it was agreed that the opening thus offered should be secured, and a joint-mission established—the Church of England sending out two or three clergy, and the American Protestant-Episcopal Church sending the same number, when practicable. The plan was afterwards expanded to embrace sending a bishop also, as head of the Mission.[1]

This suggestion having been submitted to the king, and meeting with his approval, he wrote personally to request Queen Victoria to aid in sending out a bishop of the Church of England, offering to give a site for a church and parsonage, and guaranteeing an annual income of £200 a-year, to be raised by himself and some of the foreign residents.

As it was evident that the isles could offer no more, it was agreed that funds for the Mission

---

[1] Letter from the Bishop of California to the editor of the 'Pacific Churchman,' 1866.

should be raised in England; and to this end a circular was issued, stating the case, in which the condition of the mission-field was thus summarised: "The French Roman Catholics possess a cathedral, with a bishop, clergy, &c. *The American Congregationalists also have places of worship.*"

The churches thus casually alluded to numbered, as we have seen, about 120, all erected by the voluntary contributions of the worshippers—in most cases by their own actual labour—and represented 70,000 persons, baptised since the year 1820.

The new Mission having been duly organised, the Rev. M. Staley was, on the 15th December 1861, consecrated first Bishop of the Reformed Catholic Church in Honolulu; and in the following autumn he sailed, accompanied by the Rev. G. Mason and the Rev. F. Ibbotson.

In the month of October, they reached Honolulu, where the pilot brought them the grievous tidings of the death of the Prince of Hawaii, a bright, beautiful little fellow, about five years of age. He was the only child, and his death left his parents desolate indeed.

The king seems never to have recovered from this shock, and followed his boy after one short year. He died 30th November 1863.

Even in the midst of his great sorrow, he exerted

himself to come and welcome the bishop, and told him that he had himself completed the translation, from the English Prayer Book, of the Litany, and the Morning and Evening Prayers, and that it was already in the hands of the printer.

It had been the desire of the queen that she and her son should together receive baptism at the hands of the bishop. On the 21st October, the childless mother was baptised alone, at the palace, in presence of the leading chiefs and foreign residents.

A building formerly used as a chapel was fitted up as a temporary church; and here, on the 9th November, the king and queen received the rite of confirmation.

The king appeared in the uniform of a field-marshal; Queen Emma in a white dress and long veil. The altar was vested in white, and decorated with flowers. Native men and boys had been trained to form a surpliced choir, and they chanted psalms to Gregorian tones, as they marched in procession, the king's A.D.C. carrying the bishop's banner, and his chaplain the pastoral staff.

The street was occupied by his Majesty's troops, cavalry, infantry, and rifle volunteers. The sounds of the National Anthem announced the approach of their Majesties, who knelt down as they entered the west door, to receive the Episcopal benedic-

tion. The Litany was chanted in Hawaiian, and the service made as impressive as possible.

At its close, the king and queen returned to the palace, the guns firing a royal salute, and the band playing as before.

Soon afterwards a guild was formed, " to make known the principles of the Church, as distinguished from Popery and from Calvinism; to distribute tracts, and look out persons for confirmation, and children for baptism."

In all respects the young king and queen worked heart and soul, as nursing father and nursing mother of the infant Church, never voluntarily failing to be present at any service, especially the frequent early celebrations (at 6 A.M.) of the Holy Communion.

The king was ever ready to take part in every act that implied reverence for things sacred. Thus, on Christmas eve, we hear of his joining the choristers, who walked through the town at midnight, singing carols; and, when travelling unaccompanied by a chaplain, he would robe himself in a surplice, read the Church prayers, and speak words of exhortation to the people, who, as a matter of course, flocked to hear their king, whose gentle, devoted care for them all, seemed intensified by his own great overwhelming sorrow.

In the last months of his life he worked steadily

at his translation of the Book of Common Prayer, which he had the satisfaction of completing, and to which he added a short thoughtful preface.

On the last day of November, St Andrew's Day, he died, very suddenly, at the early age of twenty-nine.

The funeral was deferred for two months, to allow time for the erection and consecration of the western wing of the present stone mausoleum. During this period the body lay in state, and crowds of residents and natives from all the isles came to pay their last homage to the dead, some wailing aloud, and others, in low monotonous tones, singing ancient *mélés*, or laments, which were taken up successively by loyal mourners.

The funeral took place on the 3d February. The church was hung with black, the coffin rested on a bier before the altar—the widowed, childless queen kneeling beside it. The Holy Communion was celebrated chorally; and almost the whole funeral service, including two beautiful chorales [1] from Mendelssohn, was chanted in Hawaiian, by a choir of fifty-two voices. Then the Dead March was played, and the procession moved on to the mausoleum in the Nuuanu valley.

The king was succeeded by his brother, who

---

[1] "I shall not in the grave remain," and "To thee, O Lord, I yield my spirit."

assumed the title of Kamehameha V. Regarding the Episcopal Mission as a sacred legacy, bequeathed by his dead brother, the new king did all in his power to make it acceptable to the people, who, however, were far too deeply attached to their own branch of the Church to tolerate any innovation.

Consequently, the principal change effected was in the management of the schools, all over the isles, which the State now took into its own hands. The bishop was made a member of the Privy Council and of the Board of Education, and to him virtually was intrusted the remodelling of the whole system. The Congregational ministers, who had created all the existing schools, found themselves deprived of all voice in the matter.

Henceforth school-attendance was made compulsory. Parents might either send their children to the common State schools, where children were taught the simpler branches of education in their own tongue; or they might send them to Government day-schools, where English was taught. The former were purely secular, as, though the Bible was read, no note or comment was allowed. The latter, on the other hand, were distinctly in connection with the Episcopal Church, and the children were encouraged to attend the daily service, —though this was optional.

Considerable care was bestowed on providing for the separate education of girls, who hitherto had for the most part attended mixed schools, where boys and girls were taught by one master. After about three years, 24 schools had been established for girls only, and 256 girls were housed in family boarding-schools.

Of the latter, the two principal schools were established at Honolulu and Lahaina, in charge of several "Sisters of Mercy," sent out by Miss Sellon in 1865. They devoted themselves heart and soul to the work they had undertaken, and by sheer goodness have succeeded in winning the respect and admiration of all parties. But their task was for several years a difficult one, and their presence in some measure reacted on the Church they strove to serve, by affording an additional proof (had any been required) of the very "High Church" nature of the Mission—a characteristic which the majority of the foreign residents disliked and dreaded exceedingly, as they do still.

The alterations in the common schools did not find favour with the people, who objected to the exclusion of religious instruction; consequently, in many villages, schools were opened in connection with the Congregational Church, independent of the Government.

About this time, the bishop attended a General

Convention of the Church at Philadelphia, bearing a letter from the king, addressed to the House of Bishops, expressive of his personal sympathy with the Episcopal Church,—"the teaching of which," he says, "seems to me more consistent with monarchy than any other form of Christianity that I have met with"—rather singular ground to select in addressing republican bishops; but the letter touched their sympathies so deeply, that they at once made arrangements to send two American clergymen to work under the bishop in Hawaii, according to the agreement made in London when the Mission was first organised.

These, and the English clergy, were established in charge of boarding-schools on each of the principal isles, and did their best to gather congregations. But these proved small indeed,—generally consisting only of the scholars, with a very small proportion of the foreign residents, who were scattered in the neighbourhood—from five to twenty persons forming the average congregations.

Even in Honolulu, where the presence and example of the king, and of the devoted widowed queen, must have exerted considerable influence, only a small fraction of the community joined the "Reformed Catholic" Church.

Now years have rolled on. The early feelings of bitterness and sectarian strife have become mellowed. The earnestness and zeal of Bishop Willis have done much to conciliate those who were at first most adverse to the Church. The present king and queen being themselves zealous Episcopalians, throw the weight of their example into the scale; but the position of the Episcopal Church in Congregational Hawaii resembles on a miniature scale that of the Episcopal Church in Presbyterian Scotland. It is a Church beloved of its own members, but altogether antipathetic to the bulk of the community.

To such foreigners as value the services of the Church in their own country, whether England or America, it is of course a most real privilege to be able to join in them, here in mid-ocean, whensoever they may chance to find themselves in the kingdom of Hawaii; and what with the facilities of travel, and the sugar-producing prospects of these isles, there is every probability that these will form a rapidly increasing body, and that whenever the long-talked-of cathedral at Honolulu is erected, it will not fail to find a full congregation.

CHAPTER XXII.

THE LAST OF THE KAMEHAMEHAS — LUNALILO THE WELL-BELOVED — HIS FUNERAL — ELECTION OF KING KALAKAUA — HIS TRAVELS — SUMMARY OF ROYAL AGE.

"THE last of the Kamehamehas" died at the close of 1872, having reigned but ten years. Though in many respects he gave proof of great capacity and vigour, and ruled with a strong hand, he was nevertheless a very different man from his excellent brother. His jovial temperament could not brook the restrictions imposed upon him by high station, and by his spiritual pastors; so he indulged in a periodical relapse to the manners and customs of heathen days.

On one of these festive occasions, he died suddenly, and various evil practices of heathendom were revived during the days of mourning.

He was the last of his race, with the exception of a half-sister, Princess Keelikolani (commonly called Ruth), whose mother was not of sufficiently high rank to entitle her to the succession.

It therefore rested with the Legislative Assembly to elect a new sovereign by ballot. Queen Emma, Prince Lunalilo, and the high chief Kalakaua, were the three candidates.

Lunalilo was the darling of the people. The son of Kekauluohi—a chiefess of the very highest rank in her own right, as the daughter of a previous dynasty, and also as being one of the queens of Kamehameha II.—he commanded the old feudal reverence of the people; while, having lived among them as one of themselves, his never-failing kindness and gentle sympathy had won for him the title of the "Well-beloved." He was said to be witty when drunk, and very wise when sober. His election was unanimous.

For one short year he reigned over the hearts of the Hawaiians, the king of their choice, responding deeply to the love which all, down to the poorest and feeblest, rejoiced to lavish on him. It was a year of gladness ever to be remembered. But, alas! the evil foreign influences which had proved the ruin of so many of his countrymen, were brought to bear on him. Constantly tempted to indulge his inborn craving for drink, he struggled bravely for a while, then yielded—and to yield was perdition.

Lacking the strength of constitution of the white men who led him on to ruin, he broke down, and perished miserably, thirteen months after his predecessor.

The grief of his people knew no bounds, and death seemed but to intensify their love. Until its cruel change had marred the beloved countenance, he lay in state at the Iolani Palace, and about ten thousand of his subjects came to look once more upon him. Beneath him was spread a priceless cloak of the royal golden feathers, which had descended to him from his mother, having for generations been a family heirloom. Now the family was extinct, and his heartbroken father, Kanaina, bade the attendants wrap the feather cloak around the dead king, ere laying him in his coffin. Thus, shrouded in the most costly fabric of the isles, he lay in state for four weeks; and though he had himself strictly forbidden all the old heathen orgies (knowing how prone to these many might be in their excess of grief), nevertheless thousands from all parts of the isles came to look upon his coffin, round which watched relays of mourners, waving the black *kahilis*, and wailing ceaselessly. They sat on the ground rocking themselves as if in dire grief, and uttering shrill cries, while singing-women chanted wild funereal dirges; and from time to time some orator would approach, and with gesticulations expressive of anguish, delivered an impassioned address, either to the dead or in his praise, to which the people responded with wails.

Nor was the mourning confined to the palace. Throughout the isles the dismal moans of sorrow were heard; bursts of passionate grief resounded from valley to valley, and echoed among the hills and rocks, as the people gathered round their watch-fires bewailing the king of their choice. Night and day the air was filled with the sound of bitter lamentation, the mournful moan, *au we! au we!* (alas! alas!)—now uttered as a loud wail, then subsiding to a low sad murmur.

When, on the 28th February 1874, the king was carried to his burial in the Nuuanu valley, the funeral-car was preceded by seventy-two *kahili*-bearers—the custom of the isles requiring that each high chief should send these, his family insignia, to do honour to his late sovereign.[1]

While this multitude of waving *kahilis* recalled olden times, modern progress was represented by

---

[1] How strangely the customs of the Eastern and Western isles recall one another! In Hawaii a multitude of feather *kahilis* are waved around the dead. In Britain nodding plumes of ostrich-feathers wave above the hearse.

In Hawaii the highest chiefs appeared on State occasions with feather-crowns and *leis;* and, in presence of their king, were required to strip to the waist. Our further advance in civilisation (though more stringent in the matter of feather head-dresses as a necessity of Court dress) only requires loyal female subjects to strip to the shoulders—a compromise which, to the lean and antiquated, is quite sufficiently trying, in the full light of noonday.

the Royal Hawaiian band playing the Dead March in 'Saul;' while 400 sailors and marines from H.M.S. Tenedos, and the American ships Benicia, Tuscarora, and Portsmouth, formed a guard of honour, and fired a salute after the coffin had been deposited in the tomb, and the religious service concluded.

The body of Lunalilo was only temporarily deposited in the Royal mausoleum. His father could not bear the thought that his bones might not be laid beside those of his beloved son. He therefore built a handsome tomb near the Kawaiahao (*i.e.*, the native church), and there both are now laid.

Once more the throne was vacant; and again, in the absence of a direct descendant of the king, a successor had to be elected. This time the choice lay between Queen Emma and David Kalakaua. The love of the people declared itself strongly in favour of the queen-dowager, who, though herself of mixed descent, was regarded as the embodiment of all that was most thoroughly Hawaiian; whereas Kalakaua, though of pure Hawaiian birth (being the son of the high chiefess Keohokalole and Kapaakea, both of whom were akin to the ancient royal family), seems to have been suspected of too strong a leaning towards foreigners.

Latterly the ever-increasing fear of foreign interference had been heightened by rash words, counselling annexation to America. Consequently, the mere suspicion of favouring such a policy secured unpopularity. "Hawaii for the Hawaiians" was the popular cry.

So the people determined that Queen Emma should reign over them; but by some adroit stratagem, matters were so conducted at the ballot in the Legislative Hall, that the election of Kalakaua was carried by thirty-nine votes in his favour, and only six for Queen Emma.

The announcement was received by the people with yells and shouts of rage. The committee deputed to carry the good tidings to the newly elected king were attacked as they left the Court House, their carriage broken up, and its fragments used as weapons of assault. The infuriated mob now besieged the Court House, shrieking for vengeance against the representatives who had deceived the people by electing Kalakaua. The native police sided with the populace; the native soldiers stood aloof, and refused to act. The windows of the house were shattered, the doors burst open, and the raging rabble rushed in and took possession.

The luckless representatives had no means of escape or of defence, so had to face the popular fury unarmed; and small pity was shown to them. Cruelly beaten and buffeted, they were thrust, bleeding and tattered, into the street, there to undergo fresh insults from the mob.

The rabble within the Court House now wreaked their blind rage on everything they could find. Desks and tables, chairs and benches, even stair-railings, were all broken up for use as weapons of offence. Valuable old law-books and documents were destroyed, and their torn fragments left soaking in pools of blood and of ink. In short, the work of devastation was complete; and none can tell to what extent the mischief might have gone, had not the marines from H.M.S. Tenedos and the U.S. ships Portsmouth and Tuscarora happily come to restore order and disperse the rioters. Foreign guards were set at all Government offices, the palace, the barracks, &c., and the storm subsided.

On the following morning the king was installed privately at his own palace, the oaths to the constitution being administered in English and Hawaiian by the chief-justice; and the Governor of Oahu, with a strong escort of Hawaiian cavalry, then visited different parts of the town and proclaimed his Majesty's accession.

Next day the king proceeded in great state to prorogue the Legislative Assembly. The wrecked Court House was restored to a semblance of order, and the poor wounded representatives assembled, looking very much like inmates of a hospital. But there was no lack of gorgeous uniforms and display, and the royal feather-mantle of the great Kamcha-meha (the only one now remaining in Hawaii) was spread over the throne, from which King Kalakaua, in a clear musical voice, read his speech, first in Hawaiian, and then in English. His name, which signifies the day of battle, seems singularly in keeping with this stormy commencement of his reign. On his return to the palace, the unstable crowd greeted him with acclamations. From that day to this, the king has reigned in peace.

By the reciprocity treaty with the United States, he has secured such a market for the produce of the isles, as has enormously increased their trade and consequent wealth; and by his own very remarkable journey round the world, he has not only made himself acquainted with other lands, but has established himself and his country in the minds of those nations in a manner hitherto undreamt of.

Going first to California, he thence sailed to Japan, where he was received with all possible honour. The emperor received him at a great banquet. So did the Club of the Nobles. The latter lasted six hours, innumerable courses of Japanese dishes being served in true native style, while scenes from the ancient Court-life of Japan were being acted on a raised platform. No expense was spared in reproducing the Court costumes of a thousand years ago, according to the best authorities. Grand theatrical performances were organised in the new theatre at Tokio, streets and gardens were illuminated (as only Japanese know how to create a fairy land), and after a long series of entertainments of every sort, King Kalakaua was conducted, with royal honours, to the limits of the empire.

Thence he passed on to Shanghai, where the mandarins met him with every demonstration of cordiality; and thence to Tientsin, where he was received by Li-hung-Chang, the generalissimo of the Chinese armies, who proposed Kalakaua's health at a grand banquet, and thanked him in the name of the Emperor of China for the just and kind treatment which all Chinese subjects have received from the Government of Hawaii.

At Hong Kong, the island king was welcomed to "British soil."

In Siam, he was received with extraordinary honours: the most sacred temples were thrown open to him; elephants with gorgeous trappings were at his service; festivals and processions—which might well seem to him as a dream too strange to be real—Siamese nautches, theatrical shows, and a great State banquet, were among the entertainments provided. Decorations were exchanged, the emperor bestowing the Order of the Rising Sun of Siam, and receiving those of Kamehameha and of Kalakaua of Hawaii.

At Singapore and Johore, at Penang and Rangoon, at Calcutta, Benares, and Bombay, English and native authorities vied in doing honour to the royal traveller. At Suez, a special train and embassy were sent by the Khedive to bring him to Cairo, whence the Khedive in person accompanied him to Alexandria.

At Cairo, Kalakaua, who is an enthusiastic freemason, delivered a lecture to the craft, which is largely represented in Honolulu, the king being a mason of the highest grade.

In the absence of the King of Italy, he was received at Naples by the Queen. From that fair city he passed to Pompeii; thence to Rome, where the Pope granted him a special audience—and we may be sure that nothing was lacking which could tend to make that reception impressive.

Then came England, and the great volunteer review at Windsor, the Castle, old Westminster, and all else of antiquity, arts, and manufactures of peace and of war that England had to show, till the weary sight-seer, and most intelligent student, was fairly exhausted.

From Manchester workshops he made a hurried visit to Edinburgh, then sped to the Continent, to France, Germany, Austria, and so on *ad infinitum,* till at length he once more found himself at rest in his own little island kingdom, full of designs for many improvements, beginning with helping and encouraging the building of the Cathedral, so long talked of,—completing and furnishing his own new Palace, and making preparations for his own coronation, and that of his queen, in true European style, and with all possible magnificence — the throne and crowns to be imported from Paris, and all the ladies of Honolulu to appear in sweeping trains and full Court dress, as worn at Buckingham Palace!

One of the chief objects the king had in view during his travels was that of encouraging desirable settlers to come to Hawaii, and there establish sugar-plantations and other industries — hoping thus, by the importation of steady and respectable men of other races, in some measure to counteract the grievous, but unmistakable, fact that the original inhabitants of the soil are fading from the earth like snow in sunshine.

Whatever may be the causes which have tended to depopulate the Hawaiian isles, it is evident that royal blood brings no exemption, for the tenure of life in the palace and in the cottage has proved alike uncertain. Within the last century no less than seven kings have ascended the throne; and of these, only two have held it for any length of time—namely, the great Kamehameha I., who died in 1819, having reigned for thirty-seven years, and Kamehameha III., who died in 1854, having reigned twenty-one years.

The stormy life of war and strong-handed action seems to have acted as an elixir on the great king; for his successors, living in peace and plenty—secure in the love of a united and prosperous people—have passed away, after short reigns of five, eight, and nine years; while that of Lunalilo, the Well-beloved, lasted but thirteen months.

The respective ages of the last five kings have been twenty-seven, forty, twenty-nine, forty-three, and thirty years. Now only one little child represents the future of the Hawaiian throne; and it is devoutly hoped that from her American parentage she may be found to have inherited the vitality which is so grievously lacking in the Hawaiian constitution. She was born in October 1875, and is the daughter of Princess Miriam Like Like, by the Honourable A. S. Cleghorn. The oppressive name wherewith this little maiden is burdened is H.R.H. the Princess Victoria-Kawekiu-Kaiulani-Lunalilo-Kalani-nuiahi-lapa-lapa.

Her third name describes her as heaven-sent. May the first she bears prove to her the earnest of a long life of prosperity and happiness.

CHAPTER XXIII.

CONCLUSION—THE RIVER OF FIRE OF 1881—THE STORY OF A GREAT DELIVERANCE.

> "Nature is but a name for an effect
> Whose cause is God. He feeds the sacred fire
> By which the mighty process is maintained,
> Who sleeps not, is not weary; in whose sight
> Slow-circling ages are as transient days."

DURING the past year the volcanic forces of Hawaii have shown unprecedented energy, and its people have endured a period of terrible suspense, while, during nine long months, the fire-floods have flowed ever nearer and nearer to their homes. At last they filled up every gulch and ravine, and still moved on and on with awful unrelenting progress, till the moving torrent of liquid rock advanced to within one mile of the town; and apparently no obstacle remained to offer even a momentary check to its onward course.

It was on the night of November 5, 1880, that

the people of Hilo observed that the clouds resting on the summit of Mauna Loa reflected that fiery glow which invariably tells of renewed action within its mighty furnace. Soon the fire-flood forced an opening for itself on the side of the mountain facing Hilo, about six miles north of the summit-crater of Mokua-weo-weo; and the fire-fountains played, and very soon formed three huge cones, one of which is about 400 feet in height, perceptibly altering the simple sweeping curve of the mountain—the outline of which is so very suggestive of the back of a stranded whale.

Meanwhile the stream poured downward till it reached the comparatively level plateau which lies between Mauna Kea and Mauna Loa, where it had space to expand; and after burning many hundred acres of forest, and filling up all the irregularities of the ground, it formed a great lake of tossing, raging fire, covering an area several miles in extent, and about fifteen in circumference, varying from 10 to 300 feet in depth.

From this great reservoir three distinct streams overflowed, each selecting a different course for its journey seaward.

As I am conscious that no words of mine can possess the thrilling interest of those of the eye-witnesses who, week by week, reported on the progress of the gruesome Fire-Dragon, I think I cannot do better than quote some passages from their letters.

Here is one to the editor of the 'Hawaiian Gazette:'—

"WAIMEA, *November* 11, 1880.

"After a hard day's toil, cutting our way through the thick forest, we pitched our tent under the lee of the hill, where we could see the whole slope of Mauna Loa. Clouds and fog had now enveloped both plain and mountain, and not a light could we see. We climbed the hillside, however, and sat down under the lee of some bushes, and awaited the clearing up of the fog and clouds. It was not long before Mauna Loa lifted its bald head above the tops of the snowy clouds, and a brilliant light burst on our view from the summit.

"In a few minutes we could see the whole line of fire along the summit, down to the terminal crater, where an intense bright light showed us that Pélé was true to herself, and was preparing a sight for all, seldom to be seen.

"As the fog gradually cleared from off the sides of the mountain, we saw a tremendous river of fire pouring down the steep sides. We could see it distinctly down the slope, till it ran into the fog-bank, which had settled like a huge snow-bed all over the lowlands. The fire was an intense white light, and was running furiously downward.

"After waiting till about eleven o'clock, and the fog not clearing off the plain, we went back down to the camp and watched the magnificent show. About half-past twelve (the fog lifting), two of us went up the side of the hill towards Puna, to see the sight. Almost under our feet lay the end of the flow, slowly pushing its way along through the scrub. The whole stream lay before us.

"Soon the moon set, and still it was light enough to see to read. Away above us in the heavens shone the brilliant fountain-head, and from thence to the end was a continuous stream of liquid lava, brighter by far than *fire*, as we could see how pale a fire looked in comparison whenever a bush blazed up alongside.

"There lay before us a stream at least thirty miles long, every inch of which was one bright rolling tide of liquid lava. There was not a single break in the whole length. It divided about a mile from the top, and ran down, forming an island, joined again, and ran five miles below. The whole front edge, about three-fourths of a mile wide, glowed with a most intensely brilliant light; and as it slowly advanced and rolled over the small trees and scrub, bright flames would flash up and die out along its whole edge.

"As we sat there in the cool still night watching it, every now and then a report as of a cannon broke on the stillness, all along the whole line of fire, caused, I suppose, by the heating of air under the new lava in the old lava-caverns, and bursting up through the crust. Occasionally a deep loud rumbling noise came from the deep recesses of the old mountain, as if it were spouting forth its fiery flood. The cannonade was very frequent, now close to us, and again, coming from a distance away up the side of the mountain.

"I could only compare the whole view with a streak of chain-lightning frozen in its tracks, as the fire seemed to come out of the heavens, it was so far above us.

"As we sat there watching it, all at once a huge dome of molten lava was thrown up about half-way up the mountain-side, and continued to flow over like an immense fountain, as long as we watched it. We also saw another stream of lava start from the fountain-head and run right along the top ridge of the mountain, for about two miles, and then apparently stop. There was no fountain throwing up lava on the top of the mountain,—only a steady rushing stream. About half-past two we descended to camp, and turned in for a few hours' sleep.

"The next day, after breakfast, we made a futile attempt to reach the flow directly opposite Kalaeeha; but as the fog and mist were very thick, we gave it up.

"On my return, I again made the ascent to the point whence we viewed the fire the night before, to determine the position of the whole flow. Before I reached the place the mists cleared off, and I had a splendid view.

"We crossed the old flow for about 1000 feet, and then stood on the very edge of that flowing *river of rock*. Oh what a sight that was! Not 20 feet from us, was this immense bed of rock slowly moving forward with irresistible force, bearing on its surface huge rocks and immense boulders, of tons weight, as water would carry a toy boat. The whole front edge was one bright red mass of solid rock, incessantly breaking off from the towering mass and rolling down to the foot of it, to be again covered up by another avalanche of white-hot rocks and sand. The height of this rock-wall varied from 12 to 30 feet.

"Along the whole line of its advance it was one crash of rolling, sliding, tumbling red-hot rock. We could see no fire or liquid lava at all, but the whole advance-line of red-hot stones and scoriæ. The latter would frequently run down the slope like water, only all separate, in red-hot grains. There were no explosions while we were near the flow,—only a tremendous roaring like ten thousand blast furnaces, all at work at once. The flow here was only *a-a*, and was so for as far as we could see it. What a tremendous heat arose from its surface! The whole mass, where no red-hot rock could be seen, was of a dull brick-colour. Its advance was very slow, but sure.

"There will not be much danger of the flow ever reaching Hilo if it should keep on running the way it is now, as it will have that immense valley to fill up below Puu Oio and Wailuku Swamp. But I am afraid that the *pahoehoe* flow will start out on the south side of the *a-a*, and then it will of course follow the 1855-56 flow to Hilo, and go quick too. So there is still great danger for our beautiful town. At present, however, it is still at a distance of twenty-one miles."

Another eyewitness wrote that the appearance of this river of *a-a* was awful beyond description, rolling, grinding, and burning its terrible way with irresistible force. The three new crater-mounds, which so materially alter the dome-like outline of Mauna Loa, lie at intervals apparently two or three miles apart, and each was a centre of active eruption.

Mr W. B. Oleson, who started from Hilo on the 15th of November to make observations, tells how he started in company with two natives for a week's tramp, in search of the lava-flow at the base of

Mauna Loa. He says: "It was a weary jaunt, over two *a-a* flows — those of 1843 and 1855. There's nothing like an *a-a* flow to take the pluck and push out of a man.

"As we came up to the black mass (which had apparently congealed throughout its whole extent), the sight was hideous. So far as could be seen, there was an indescribable tumble of *a-a*, from ten to twenty feet high, having almost perpendicular sides, so that it seemed ready to crash down on us as we stood next to it. We succeeded in getting on to the flow, though we had to move briskly in some places, not on account of steam or smoke, but because of a dry heat that told us plainly enough that the lava was all molten beneath us.

"At one point we had a fine view either way, showing the direction and nature of the flow. Several steam-holes could be seen, but no fire. The flow had run down the mountain-side from near the summit in several streams—all, however, uniting below.

"On Thursday morning, at about one o'clock, we began the ascent of Mauna Kea. Before daylight we had some magnificent views of the great crater of Mokua-weo-weo and the subsidiary crater on the eastern slope. Two broad streams, like twin rivers, were flowing down the mountain through the night, not extending, however, more than half a mile, when they seemed to go underground. Evidently from the point where these streams disappeared, one or more conduits conducted the lava to the very front of the flow. This seemed to be verified when, on our return to Hilo, we had passed Kipukaahina, and found that the lava had pushed ahead several miles.

"On Thursday afternoon a new phenomenon appeared. After our return to camp, we saw a huge column of smoke, 600 or 700 feet high, rising vertically a mile to the north of all previous points of action. At night, fire was seen at the base of the column, gradually increasing in size and intensity, and on Friday night and Saturday morning the crater proper and this point of eruption seemed to have united, and a great glare of fire and clouds of smoke could be seen with the centre of activity moving toward the north.

"The lava has flowed about twenty-five miles toward Hilo, and is now twenty miles away. It is from a quarter to half a mile wide at the upper part of its course, and from three-quarters to a mile wide at the lower end. It has entered the woods on one side; and as it rises high above the 1855 flow, which is specially high at this point, its front looks threatening enough.

"I did not see any portion of it in motion at the lower end, but conclude that the motion was at the centre, and of a rotary nature, rolling the masses of *a-a* and clinkstone to either side in great piles as it rushed along. I found *ohia*-trees not more than ten feet high, with the stalk buried in the *a-a*, while the foliage had not lost its natural colour, though showing some effects of the heat. These were always at the lower end of the perpendicular sides, showing that the congealing masses had been thrown to one side as the stream moved along."

. . . . . .

As seen from afar, a canopy of flaming light seemed to overhang the mighty dome of Mauna Loa; and torrents of fire, of intense brightness, streamed down its slopes, till they were lost to sight in a dense bank of clouds, which overspread the base of the mountain.

One of those who visited the scene, has described his first glimpse of that brilliant flame-head as seen against the star-lit heavens, and the stream of liquid lava, three-fourths of a mile in width, which rolled along at a white heat for thirty miles, accompanied by flashing gleams and intermittent detonations, suggestive of heavy cannonading. While he watched the awful summit, a second torrent boiled over, and flowed along the ridge in a steady rushing stream, extending for about two miles.

With painful toil, he crossed a former lava-flow,

till he stood within twenty feet of a scene which he compared to hell broken loose—where avalanche after avalanche of fire poured down, in volume, from twenty to thirty feet deep, and from one to two miles in width, of rolling, tumbling, gliding, red-hot rock, liquid lava, scoria, and sand, a molten river, bearing on its surface huge rocks and boulders weighing many tons—all grinding onward with a dull continuous roar. The heat was terrific, and the surface, as it cooled, changed from a white heat to a dull brick-colour.

At more distant points, the lava seems to have found subterranean channels, and its course was only betrayed by the extraordinary phenomena of rock-ridges upheaved without apparent cause,—just as garden-mould, thrown up in hillocks and ridges, reveals the secret mining and burrowing of a busy mole. As the mighty volcanic stream tunnelled its secret path, a heaving movement of the surface indicated its direction, and here and there banks of hard black lava, perhaps a hundred feet in width by twenty in height, were observed quietly to glide away, as if suddenly seized with a desire to travel!

At times the land was so enveloped in dense clouds of smoke, that vessels nearing Hawaii could not discern the land. On the 16th November, the schooner Pauahi lay to, off Honokaa, while its boat rowed to shore—a distance of three miles. It was not until the third day that the boat was able to return, the schooner being shrouded in dark smoke. About 4 P.M. it became less dense, and the captain and crew distinctly beheld a submarine eruption of scoriæ and rocks at a distance of a quarter of a mile ahead of the ship. The sea seethed and boiled, clouds of steam and masses of pumice were thrown up as in a fountain, and the display lasted about three minutes. In much alarm, the captain prepared to retreat; but a moment later, a similar submarine eruption was observed astern, so there was little to be gained by flight. The sea, meanwhile, was tossing unquietly, causing the vessel to roll heavily.

On the 1st of December, Judge Hitchcock (from whose letter of the 11th November I have already quoted) again started from Hilo to reconnoitre. "That night," he says, "we encamped on high ground, where we could see the whole mountain side and slope. But before dark a heavy fog set in and shut out all our view. About midnight, however, it cleared off, and we had a magnificent display. The summit-line of fire from Mokua-weo-weo to the terminal crater was extremely active, and we saw a stream of fire flowing down, as we supposed then, along the old line. It was widely spread out, but toward the last it divided into two main streams. The sight from our camp was splendid, and the view was unobstructed by fog or cloud.

"We struck the first flow about two miles from the lava end, and found it still hot and smoking along the edges, and in places all over the surface. We struck straight across it, however, dodging the hotter places, and in just half an hour descended the south side into the *a-a*[1] of 1856, and from thence down to the *pahoehoe* flow of the same year. The new *a-a* flow was at that place a little over half a mile wide, and terribly uneven. It had almost entirely covered over the *a-a* of 1856, and in some places even had overflowed the *pahoehoe* stream.

"We then turned our course in a straight line for the most northern of the two streams. Our way for the first five miles was altogether across the old *pahoehoe*. Our ascent by this time was quite steep and tiresome; and after about five miles farther of that slow travel, we at last stood alongside of the flow, whose red-hot sides even the light of the sun did not dim, at more than a mile distance. This flow was narrow, not over two or three hundred feet in width.

"We were now within about ten miles of the new crater formed during the last few days. It is

---

[1] *A-a*, the very roughest black lava, forming huge blocks; *pahoehoe*, smooth lava.—*Vide* vol. i. p. 133.

evidently formed of volcanic scoriæ and sand, as the sides were very steep and even. Its height may be about 350 feet. The *a-a* flow, alongside of which we now stood, was slowly moving down the slope, in the same manner as described in my former account, red-hot rocks parting off from the steep sides and rolling to the bottom, setting fire to every shrub and tree they touched, only in turn to be again covered by another avalanche of the same. The steam and gases arising from the flowing mass were almost entirely free from the smell of sulphur—so much so, that at a few yards distance one could breathe them. The smell was somewhat like that arising in a large iron-foundry when the molten iron is flowing into the moulds.

"After a while, we started across to view the other stream, whose incessant avalanche of rock seemed to betoken great activity; and on climbing a spur of old *a-a*, what a sight met our gaze! About 100 feet from us, the new *a-a* had reached the precipitous side of the old flow, and was rushing down the steep incline like a river. This was *a-a* in a fluid or semi-fluid state. It was just fluid enough to run, and that was all. The stream was about fifty feet in width, and came slowly but irresistibly down towards a small island of rocks where we were standing.

"Its surface was nearly on a plane, but entirely

covered with small spear-like projections, standing up and out of the liquid lava, while the surrounding lava was red hot, and in a semi-fluid state.

"In this the flow of *a-a* differs greatly from *pahoehoe*, which flows unevenly, but with a smooth glittering surface. Again, *a-a*, even when flowing, looks like rock granulated all the way through. It has no cohesion, and when falling, breaks up into small pieces, and hardens almost instantly.

"It is quite singular that up to this time no *pahoehoe* has been ejected during this eruption, only *a-a*.

"While watching the flow of this *a-a* stream, we saw a huge boulder, loosened from the mass above, come rolling down the stream, pushed on by the irresistible power behind. It rolled completely over, exposing its white-hot surface, and then again sank almost out of sight, only to be upheaved again.

"After watching that grand sight a few minutes longer, we commenced retracing our steps; and just before dark, after following down the first *a-a* flow, keeping it on our right, we reached Halealoha just before dark, after a weary tramp of over twenty-five miles."

. . . .

Six months glided on, and still the fiery streams continued to grind on their seaward way, burning the forest through which they passed, filling up ravines, and making for themselves a vast level highway, and in places huge tunnels, through which the liquid lava flowed. It became evident that, should the awful streams unite, there would soon remain no trace of Hilo or of its harbour.

The 'Hawaiian Gazette' of July 6th says:—
"The past week has been one of great excitement in Hilo, in consequence of the renewed activity in the volcanic fires on Mauna Loa. One arm of the fiery stream has pushed itself into the Kukuau gulch, and is within three miles of the village of Hilo. All Hilo may be said to have visited the flow during the last few days. Men, women, and children, some on foot and some on horseback, have made the pilgrimage.

"As seen on Wednesday, June 29th, it presented a view never to be forgotten. A mile above the lower end of the stream, the lava was flowing in a liquid living torrent, some 30 feet wide along its course, consuming everything in its way. From this point, about half a mile of the seething, surging torrent could be seen. The belt covered with lava was some 500 feet wide, all hot, and liable at any moment to break out into renewed activity. At night the scene was awfully grand. The sky has been brilliantly illuminated for nights past with the reflected glare.

"Many in Hilo have been packing during the past few days, so as to be ready to make a sudden start, should the lava-stream turn a little more Hilowards. Nevertheless, buying and selling, and all the routine of busy life, go on as usual.

"An auction of real estate was held at Hilo on Saturday, June 25th. Two lots of land belonging to the estate of the late S. Kipi were sold. Bidders were few, and the bidding far from spirited. One lot, of an acre and a half, brought only about 220 dols., which had been valued at 900 dols. per acre; and a two-acre lot, in a most desirable part of the village, with small house on it, sold for only 280 dols. Two years ago this land could not have been purchased for 2000 dollars."

On the 30th June, Mr Hitchcock wrote from Hilo as follows: "Last Wednesday the mountain was observed to be more than usually active, the whole summit crevasse pouring forth immense volumes of smoke. By Friday noon the three southern arms had all joined into one, and rushing into a deep but narrow gulch, forced its way down the gulch in a rapid flow. By Saturday noon, it had run a mile, and was just above John Hall's house on the south side. On Monday morning it was reported to have reached the flats, back of Halai hills.

"My wife and I started that afternoon with the intention of spending the night beside the flow.

We met crowds of people returning thence, and all reported it active, and coming rapidly down the gulch. We rode up to it before dark, and found that the stream was entirely confined to the gulch, and intensely active. The flow was from 10 to 30 feet in depth, and the whole frontage was one mass of liquid lava, carrying on its surface huge cakes of partly cooled lava. Soon after we reached it, the flow reached a deep hole, some 10 or 15 feet in depth, with perpendicular sides. The sight, as it poured over that fall in two cascades, was magnificent. The flow was then moving at the rate of about 75 feet an hour.

"About midnight we noticed a diminution in the activity of the gulch-flow, and soon saw a bright red glare above the tree-tops, and were presently startled by the burning *gas bursts*, and the crackling and falling of the trees somewhere above us. The whole sky above us was lined with the light of burning trees and shrubs.

"About 2 A.M. we made the attempt to reach the scene of the great activity, and succeeded by going up the south side of the gulch some quarter of a mile. And what a scene lay before us as we ascended a slight elevation! The on-coming overflow had swept over the banks of the narrow gulch, and was flowing like water into a dense grove of *neneleau* and guava trees. There they stood in a sea of liquid lava, over a space of more than an acre, while the fires were running up their trunks, and burning the branches and leaves overhead. The flow was so rapid that the trees were not cut down.

"In one place we saw a huge dome of half-melted lava rise up, 15 or 20 feet high, and twice that in diameter, and apparently remain stationary, while the fiery flood went on.

"It is almost impossible to say now when the flow will reach the sea; but all things considered, the probability is, that it will take the Kukuau Gulch. It is now not over $1\frac{3}{4}$ mile from the sea. Probably, before you hear from us again, all the lower part of the town will be destroyed."

Two days previously, the Rev. Titus Coan thus described the progress of the eruption: "For a few days past our volcanic fires have been more vivid and glaring than ever. The line of fire extends for miles from north-west to south-east.

"The northern line is less than six miles from us, and the south-eastern is less than five miles distant.

"From the south-east the seething fusion has fallen into a rough water-channel, 20 to 50 feet wide, which comes down from the main bed of the flow almost direct to Hilo, crossing Volcano Street, half a mile from Mills's store, and entering into the Waialama stream, which cuts the beach about midway. In this way the lava, at white heat, is fast approaching the shore. It is now only two and a-half miles from Volcano Street, and it is very liquid, running much like water. It has, some part of the time, run at the rate of half a mile a day.

"Large parties of fifty to one hundred visit it daily, and some go up early in the morning and return, and again go up in the afternoon. Mr Kennedy and Mr Richardson are alarmed for the mills, and they have begun to pack and remove their valuable articles. Our town is greatly moved, and some have suspended all other business to watch the fires. The puffs of smoke and steam along the descending channel appear like the smoke of steamers descending a river. The main body of the fire is moving slowly down upon us in sufficient breadth to sweep our whole town, while the small stream is like advanced pickets on a skirmish-line.

"*Tuesday, June 28th,* 5 P.M.

"Mrs Coan and I have been to the lava-flow to-day. We found two streams of liquid lava coming down in rocky channels, which are sometimes filled with roaring waters, but are nearly dry at this time. These two gulches are too small to hold the seething fusion, and the fiery flood overruns the banks, and spreads out on either side. The united width of these streams may vary from 50 to 200 feet. In going down the steeper parts of these rocky beds, the roar is like that of our Wailuku river, or our surf, and often like thunder.

"Probably a few days hence we shall see its triumphant entrance into our town, about half a mile east of Church Street. It will be a grand spectacle, though full of terror. If the vast fiery lines which seam the hill behind us, only five or six miles distant, do not move down upon us, we may hope that most of our town will be spared; but of this we are not assured. We wait the will of Him whose wisdom and will are perfect, and we plead His mercy, which is infinite."

Mrs Coan writes :—

"HILO, *June* 27, 1881.

". . . When we reached the turn in the road on the Puna side of the cemetery, there burst suddenly upon our view the spot to which the fire had progressed. And it looked alarmingly near—not more than a mile distant; but as we rode on, the distance increased, and we found we went two miles or more beyond the farther of the three crater-hills.

"A few rods of walking after we dismounted brought us to the margin of the stream—no limpid, sparkling brook, such as one might have looked for in that lovely emerald oasis, but a red-hot, death-dealing flow of lava. Years ago, people lived thereabouts, and the land was under much cultivation. You can easily imagine what luxuriant growth of grass there would be, and what strong, leafy guava-bushes, in what had become almost swampy land since the soil-tillers had abandoned it. But right over this freshness and beauty the flood was coming.

"We pressed on till we reached a rocky gorge, down which, in heavy rains, a perfect torrent rushes to the sea. This gorge is now nearly dry, except here and there pools of water in its deepest hollows; and the lava falls in a red-hot, gory mass, where aforetime cool cascades sparkled and rippled. Here we found crowds of natives and some foreigners watching the wild scene.

"We were told that others were still farther on, where the main branch was; we had seen only overflows from that which was filling up a still larger channel. A native volunteered to guide us through the bushes and over the great rocks; but we had progressed only a few yards, when word came that the stream in the narrow gorge was moving on so fast that our return was likely to be cut off; and Mr Coan, marking its advance by the smoke that rose, felt it was not wise to attempt to go to the farther side.

"Meantime, the gentlemen who were already

there took note of the warning, and retraced their steps; but Mr W. offered to assist me to a place where I could see it safely; and what I saw was the most awe-inspiring sight of all, for the mass was far heavier and wider spread, and for speed and fury of motion it was like the rapids of Niagara.

"What terrific pouring out of fusion there must be to supply these several streams—their advanced posts—and to make them so lively so far from the fountain! Why, at night it shows an emblazoned front extending for between four or five miles.

"I grieve for the lovely ferns,—one moment waving their fresh fronds in the breeze—the next, scorched by the heat, then reduced to ashes.

"The roar of the lava was something fearful: it was as the roar of a flood. Then the detonations—ten in a minute, as timed by the watch—and some of the explosions so heavy, we felt the ground tremble under us.

"While we lingered in the gorge, there came an alarm from the natives, to the effect that the flow was approaching the spot where the horses were tied, and that soon the road would be cut off. One of the party called it a false alarm; but then, the flow was breaking out here and there so rapidly, from over the banks of the channel which it had filled up, no wonder it seemed to some that the danger was everywhere.

"It was now noon; and we sat down to rest on a prostrate trunk, thick green grass under our feet, and verdant boughs of trees above us, but behind the advancing stream. Here the ground was very level, and of course the flow was not rapid; but foot by foot, yard by yard, it rolled forward, and very soon after we had left our seat, the burning ruin covered the ground on which our feet had rested, and the log was aflame.

"There was intense fascination in watching all the movements, at whatever point we were,—sometimes it was the quick cooling over of the surface, forming the corrugated ridges that characterise *pahoehoe*, and glistening in the sun like perfect bronze — sometimes the puffing of great bubbles, that crusted over a moment, then sank back into the fiery bosom from which they had risen. Then the lava rushed down steep places, and filled up the hollows, from which wreaths of steam curled up; and then it crept through the dense grass, where, for a moment, the verdure hung like a green canopy over the red serpent, which glided under, to melt away and be seen no more.

"We turned to leave the scene, with the prayer that we might never see it doing greater damage than this.

"As we looked over the town of Hilo to the gleaming sea, the prospect was one of entrancing beauty, with emerald rice-fields and *taro* patches, sugar-plantations, and the Waiakea sugar-mill. We grieved at the thought of the black desolation that will mar the scene should the fire-flood sweep through it. Yet we may well be thankful that no lives are actually endangered.

"It seems plain that our homes are not to be overwhelmed from this side; and we will still trust that the stream which threatens us on the right shall in due time be stayed, obedient to the command, 'Hitherto shalt thou come, but no farther.'

"A prayer-meeting was held that evening at Mr Lyman's. We found comfort in singing the sweet old hymns, and I believe that we were able from our hearts to say, 'Thy will be done.'"

The next letters we received from Hilo bore date July 4, 1881. From them we learnt that the fate of the town still trembled in the balance, though the danger grew hourly more imminent. Slowly but steadily the awful river of molten rock flowed nearer and more near—a terrible moving wall, ever gliding onward.

The flow had then divided into several streams, one of which was advancing directly towards the sea. The town lay exactly in its course. Many of the inhabitants had already forsaken their homes, and all were prepared for flight at a moment's notice.

The danger most dreaded was not merely the slow progress of the ever-advancing wall, but the far more sudden destruction that must result, should that comparatively thin crust give way and open the flood-gate of the fiery torrent thus pent back, but which would then burst forth in an awful resistless flood.

This flow was now taking a course directly towards the main street, so that such an outburst would inevitably overwhelm the greater part of the town.

Another flow had shaped its course for the homestead of Waiakea, the plantation of Mr Davies, the British vice-consul. Like that which threatened Hilo, the flow was advancing like a gigantic wall; but on the morning of Sunday, 26th August, a stream of fiery lava, liquid as water, and glowing with a white heat, broke from the face of the flow and rushed tumultuously down a narrow and tortuous gulch about a mile in length. Its course was so impetuous that two gentlemen who had gone up to report on the advance of the flow escaped with the utmost difficulty.

At the foot of the gulch is a hollow, which is often filled with water, forming a lagoon. By the end of the week the lava had entirely filled this bed, and proceeded to overflow the alluvial flat around, causing serious destruction of valuable arable land.

The fields of growing sugar-cane, however, being for the most part on a higher level than that now reached by the lava, escaped; but the mill and other plantation-buildings were in imminent danger.

All portable stores were removed, and the manager took measures to be in readiness to remove the plant itself to a place of safety at the last moment — rather a risky delay, but one which was justified by the necessity of carrying on the work of crushing with the utmost vigour, in order to get as much as possible done towards saving the ripe canes. Otherwise this valuable crop would have been entirely lost.

There was still a hope that the mill might escape, as there were two outlets for the destructive flood. One of these was a gulch, by which the lava might pass onward to the sea, filling up the deep course of the Waiolana stream, but doing comparatively little damage. The other outlet was by the shallow gulch of Kukuao. Had the lava selected this channel, it would almost inevitably have overflowed the level ground and destroyed the sugar-mill and plantation-buildings.

The letters that were penned by those actually on the spot were truly voices from the midst of the fires.

One correspondent says: "We walked upon the hot surface of the lava for perhaps a quarter of a mile from the end, seeing a good deal of action or flowing lava at various points along the banks. This flow is composed entirely of the *pahoehoe* or satin lava, and every crack and fissure glowed with the fire beneath, and we had to step constantly, to keep our shoes from burning.

"The surface seemed to be as hot as the top of a stove while cooking, and a camping-party that we visited cooked all their food on the lava, and boiled a tea-kettle in a few minutes over a steam-crack. I visited the flow four times, and can never forget the impression made during a visit at night a week after the first view.

"The stream of lava had advanced full half a mile since the first visit, and was coming down the water-course towards Waiolana. The liquid lava came slowly rolling over the rocks and into the pools of water, causing it to boil and the steam to rise in a fearful manner. The heat is intense, and the crowd of natives and foreigners is constantly receding as the fiery flood advances. During my stay of two hours, I should think the flow had advanced over 200 feet.

"During the afternoon some of my friends had seen the molten lava run over a fall of perhaps 15 feet into the water below, 6 feet deep, and the sight was grand beyond description. There was quite a large basin to be filled with lava, and it took an hour and forty-two minutes to fill it up even, before it could continue on its course.

"The end of the stream is constantly surrounded by a crowd of men, women, children, and even dogs, and the boys are busy in getting out specimens of soft lava, which they make into vases and other curiosities.

"There is a wonderful fascination in watching the progress of this fiery mass as it advances with such slow but irresistible force—covering all the rocks, filling up ravines, licking up pools or streams of water, like some dread monster from the infernal regions.

"It is now within two miles and a half of Hilo; and if it continues to flow as at present, it will certainly reach the bay in a few weeks, probably between the town and the Waiakea mill. The flow most dreaded by those in Hilo, however, is the main one, still in or near the woods, perhaps six miles distant, and which seems to be quite active. This flow would probably pass to the north of the Halai hills, in which case it would take in the whole of the town, and ruin the beautiful Bay of Hilo.

"Let us all devoutly pray that the action at the source may entirely cease."

Another says: "On Tuesday, 26th July, we took our tent, and went up as a family, to camp out, and see the grand sight of a night-view. We sent

E., F., and K. ahead with pack-animals, and they made a good selection of a site for the tent, and when F. and I arrived after five o'clock P.M., the tent was all pitched.

"It was on a hill overlooking the flow, only a few feet distant, and took in a range of a mile or more; and when the night shut in, the whole distance was lighted up with the volcanic fires, with burning bushes, and trees, and grass, to add to the variety. It was the most fearful sight I ever witnessed. The sight is heightened ten thousandfold by night, for it brings out light at every crack, where only smoke is seen by day. It would take a mightier pen than mine to describe it.

"One very wonderful thing is the sight of a shower of rain on the hot lava, so strange is the effect produced by the varying shades of the clouds of smoke. One will be as black as darkness itself, then another of a lighter colour, down to the clearest, purest white. After the cloud is lifted, everything on fire seems to burst out afresh with brighter light, and to rush on with greater speed, flames lapping up the drops of water as if only heightened by it. You can *imagine* anything. Flames dance out in the distance by groups or singly, suggestive of infernal spirits beckoning, and dancing, and rushing, fanning themselves with flame.

"Lights of deepest red are mingled with blue,

green, and white, flashing sometimes like lightning. Fortunately for us, there was a strong land-breeze all night, which kept us free from the fumes, though occasionally I did smell sulphur. Our tent was so secure, there was no need to move away during the night. We had frequent showers, but did not suffer from dampness.

"We could not see the end of the flow, and did not learn how far it progressed during the night; but it was active all over, bursting out and flowing on itself over and over again, piling up and filling in.

"The day we came down (Wednesday, 27th) there was a great outbreak at John Hall's place. The children stayed to take down the tent, and they said there were three reports like thunder before they came down, in that direction. Mr S. and others went right up there, and saw the whole spot rise up and then burst out, flowing all around from the centre, making a kind of crater there.

"This John Hall is the only one as yet that has lost his home by the lava. He is a man of much heathenism, believing in old traditions—a sort of *kahuna* (sorcerer). He had put up flags around his place, and said that Pélé would not dare to pass those; but he has been obliged to leave, though he stayed so long, it was almost feared he would be swallowed up. It does seem strange that that spot should be the centre of so much activity."

The long-continued anxieties of these terrible months have betrayed various lingering traces of old Hawaiian superstition among the old folk, who were supposed to have entirely put away every trace of heathendom. Here is a sketch by a native of the isles, published in the Hawaiian paper, *Elele Poakolu*:—

"The devastating lava had been for some time threatening the homestead of one Keoni Holo, an old native, who had lived for thirty years on a pleasant *kuleana* of about twelve acres, flourishing with well-irrigated *taro* patches, potato patches, and choice fruit-trees, within a short distance of Hilo.

"Keoni had faith that, although great Pélé might not heed the prayers of foreigners, she would be touched by the offerings of a true *keiki* (son) of the soil. He offered his choicest pig to the advancing flood of fire, crying out: '*Aloha o Pélé! Mohai ia oe o Pélé!*' (Hail to thee, O Pélé! Receive my gift, O Pélé!) And the dread goddess responded with a puff of steam and a crackling flow of blood-red fire, that smothered the squeak of the poor porker.

"Again Keoni stood before the advancing tide of fire, and offered chickens, *ohia* fruits, *ohelo* berries, and a lock of his hair; but Pélé was not to be coaxed by Keoni. Her cohorts of red wrath moved onward, licked up with a moment's fizzle the growing *taro* patches, crackled through the orchard, and with a flash and a flicker, rolled over the old man's once smiling homestead, leaving overspread above its site the burning floor of an inferno, a surface of twisted, serpentine folds, and coils of glassy black lava."

Such lingering reverence for the ancient fire-goddess was not confined to the lower orders. One fine old chiefess (commonly called Ruth), who holds, or held, official rank as governess of one of the isles, went in person to the flow, and presented offerings of silk handkerchiefs and bottles of brandy to Pélé, praying her, if she had any *aloha* (i.e., love) for her, to go back to the mountains.

This occurred only a few days before the fires began to subside, so of course this loyal disciple of Pélé assumes this happy result to be a clear proof that her offering was accepted.

From the date of these letters a fortnight elapsed ere another mail brought us tidings from the friends whose peaceful and beautiful town was thus endangered. There was too much reason to fear that their homes must have been abandoned, and that the sweet gardens of fragrant blossom and graceful bamboos, which but a few months ago filled us with admiration and delight, probably lay buried beneath the lava-flood, or, at best, stood scarred and scathed by the fiery breath of the stream, as it burnt its seaward way, to empty its exhaustless store of molten rock into the harbour.

With thankful wonder, then, we received the glad news that the danger was past—that the stream had ceased to flow, and that Hilo and its people were safe. As in many another boon, vouchsafed to believing prayer, this seemed almost too marvellous to be true; yet so it was.

That man's extremity is God's opportunity is an old saying, yet ever new, and here it was once more proven. For when the people of Hilo had almost quite given up hope, they appointed a solemn day of humiliation, on which they assembled together, that all might with one voice up-raise the prayer which had for months been ascending from many a heart and many a household, though its answer had been so long delayed.

But now all agreed to meet, and plead that if it so pleased the Lord, their homes might be spared. All places of business were closed, and crowded services were held at morning, noon, and evening in all the churches — Catholic and Protestant, native and foreign—throughout the district.

Even the "stranger within their gates" joined in that solemn act of worship; for the Chinamen, who had burnt their joss-sticks, and made offerings to the fire-demons, all in vain, came in a body to attend the evening service at the Hawaiian church, that they might test the power of the Christian's God.

We may leave it to those materialists who deny the overruling hand of the Creator in the wonderful working of the great forces of nature, to search out purely natural causes for the strange coincidence that, *from that very hour, the fire-flood was stayed.* The great fountain on the mountain-top ceased to flow, and the stream, which for nine long months had been steadily moving seaward, suddenly stood still, and thenceforth did not advance one foot. There it now remains, an abiding monument of the appalling danger and of the miraculous deliverance.

Many months must elapse ere that vast mass of solid rock becomes cool throughout; but the upper surface very soon hardened, and allowed eager and wondering visitors to walk over it, as on a strange new roadway towards the mountains.

On the 14th August, Mrs Luther Severance wrote to me as follows:—

"I know you are longing to hear about our lava-flow. You will thank the Lord, as we do, that it has ceased action; for such a danger, within fifteen minutes' walk from town, was too near for comfort. It had advanced to within a mile from the beach, having travelled fully forty miles from the summit of Mauna Loa.

"We hardly can think or talk of anything else. This fiery flood, whose steady advance we have watched since last November—that is, for nine long months—has occupied all our thoughts, and for the last two months we have spent much of our time near this terrible, fascinating monster: night and day has called us to its side.

"I wish you could have witnessed with us its wonderful contortions, the lava twisting and writhing like some weird nightmare of myriad twining snakes. We have witnessed this awful dragon with its breath of fire, burning forest-trees, leaping over precipices, licking up green grass and ferns with its flaming tongues, drinking up pools of water, leaving desolation and destruction behind it. It lies outstretched a mile in width, just at the back of the three little extinct craters behind the town.

"If it had run a few days longer, it would have come down near the jail, and must have spread over the lower part of the town. It is hard to realise that it is dead: not cold yet—indeed the heat is still very great, and fire can be seen in some places through the cracks; but it is lifeless, and our long anxieties and fears are at an end.

"We were in great danger one night. A party of us went up in the afternoon. We found so little fire at the outer edge, that we ascended the flow itself for a considerable distance, stepping on such hot lava that it would have been dangerous to stand still. We were so carried away by the sights all around us, that we did not realise how dark it was growing, till suddenly the rain fell in torrents, striking the hot lava, and forming steam so dense that we could not see a foot ahead of us.

"We could only stand still. If we moved, we might step into a fiery crack where, only a few feet from us, a stream of fire six feet broad was rushing along. All around us and beyond us, as far as the eye could reach, stretched black lava, illuminated with starry lights, revealing the molten sea that lay below. Trees were crackling and burning; we felt suffocated with the smoke, steam, and gas: in short, our situation was most perilous. It was so dark that we could not see what direction to take. The lava was so hot that we stood first on one foot, then on the other, and there was danger that the block on which we stood would crack off and subside into the fiery flood.

"When the rain ceased, we rushed along, often falling in our haste, till we were again stopped by the rain. Little fiery tongues darted out all around us: it was a weird, strange scene. The steam was so dense that we could hardly see one another, and even the fires were dimmed by the rain. But the kind Father, to whom we looked, guided us, and finally we reached a little island surrounded on all sides by lava; but it felt cool to our feet, and we rejoiced. When the moon rose about midnight, a way of escape was found, and we thanked God for our deliverance."

Mr W. R. Castle gives the next report:—

"HILO, *August* 25, 1881.

"To all appearances the great eruption of 1880-81 is at an end. The people of Hilo do not say much, but are silently and infinitely relieved. During all these terrible months since the lava-flow began its steady march to the sea from the depths of the woods, there has not been much said; but a feeling of suspense, in view of the approach of this infernal destroyer, has oppressed the minds of all. And now, at the very doors of the town, the grim foe has been arrested, by the withdrawal of the force behind.

"The courage and patience of the people have been most admirable. What would long ere now have produced a terrible panic in Honolulu, has been met here with a patient waiting. If, however, any suppose that the flow has lost its interest, it is a great mistake. For months to come it must prove intensely attractive. It is in many respects the most interesting flow on record in these islands.

"We greatly desired to trace out the sources of

the flows variously known during the past few months as Laumaia flow, the Hilo and Puna branches; so, having previously despatched a well-laden mule through the woods to the lower line of the flow of 1853, we started off for a long and hard trip. Leaving our horses at some *kukui*-trees on the great flat above the Halai hills, we struck across the country to the flow at the natural bridge. This bridge no longer exists, as the lava flowed over and covered it, and then pushed its way up the cool stream to the north. The flow itself, however, makes a natural bridge, as the large volume of water in this stream continues to flow from under the new lava, and yet has no visible outlet.

"From the natural bridge the flow curves away round to the south-west, and thence up to John Hall's, where there are several blow-holes. Going up the flow, we came to a sharp hill, down which the lava had poured furiously, through a narrow space of not over 1000 feet wide. It was densely covered with fallen trees, cut off but not burned, as the flow which burned them off at the base had not been followed by an overflow. At the head of this flow we came out upon a vast field of lava to the west and north.

"Turning to the right, and following the line of woods, we came to the upper line of the so-called

Laumaia flow; and we followed that till nightfall overtook us near the Laumaia house—a comfortable hut made of *koa* bark, and weather-proof.

"The Laumaia house is on the 1856 flow, and was seriously threatened in the rear with the new lava-flow, which came to within 300 feet of it. We passed a cool night at this superb mountain-retreat, and awoke with the break of day, to partake of a hasty breakfast. Then sending the boys down through the woods home, we started again up the flow, the Laumaia branch.

"Before we reached the head, Mauna Loa appeared in full view, and from the great source-crater could be seen a heavy column of smoke ascending to a great height. Below this crater, to the left, could be seen the mound where the second crater sends forth the flow of this year; columns of smoke and steam marked the whole line of flow from the top to where we stood.

"Climbing a low mound, we overlooked a level lake of lava, three miles in extent, which must in places be fully 200 feet deep. Here in the early spring stood dense forest, all of which was burned by the lava-flow.

"I must mention here, that across a hot crack, we met with one of our large well-known spiders, with a beautiful web, watching for strangers. To the nearest line of wood was about three-quarters of a mile, and the lava was still hot; yet here he was, ready for business.

"We constantly heard the boom of a subterranean explosion. The surface was cracking, and our poles took fire at almost every crack. In some places we saw the live fire, and could not but think with a horrible shudder that the weight of our own bodies trampling over the roof of the cavern must suffice to make the infernal archway collapse and precipitate us into its consuming abyss. But we ran over its roof, with a thickness of but little more than a foot, or even less, between our feet and this fiery tunnel, and it gave us no sign of yielding.

"However, it is to be presumed that as the heat decreases, the mass of overarching rock will contract and become more brittle, and will consequently splinter and crack, and in many cases fall in. On the whole, I was impressed with the feeling that we were walking over a dying flow. . . ."

Eerie and horrible accounts are given by various men, who, braving the blasts of hot air which still poured out through the blow-holes, ventured to peer through these cavities into the awful region below. The so-called blow-hole is simply a spot where the thin lava-crust has broken in, leaving a ragged hole 12 or 15 feet in diameter, affording a glimpse of the strange tunnels formed by the lava itself, and which became the conduits through which the fire-streams flowed. Some of these tunnels are very deep, and some are riddled with great holes, showing where the running lava has receded still lower, so that in some places it is possible to look through a vista of successive depths (as into the Seven Hells of Buddhism) and see the lower levels of terrific heat and furnace-like glow of these truly infernal regions.

The air issuing from the blow-holes was so hot as to inflame pieces of wood thrown into it; and pieces of black lava thrown into the tunnel soon became glowing red, though the stream had quite ceased to flow. From one point the spectators could obtain a perfect view along the interior of the tunnel for a distance of about 200 feet, and could see that its floor was formed of huge rounded boulders, as if it had originally been the bed of a rocky water-course, which was evidently the case. Even the intense heat to which they had been subjected had not sufficed to melt these, though they were still glowing in the incandescent heat.

On either side of this water-worn causeway rise walls of glowing lava, arching inwards so as to form a canopy; and here and there some mass of rock forms a huge column, as if to give greater support to the immense slabs of smooth *pahoehoe* which form the roof.

These blow-holes seem to be invariably found on

the slopes of falling ground, with a rapid decline for a considerable distance below them, which, by allowing the molten fluid to drain away and leave the tunnel empty, removed the support from the upper crust, which, on cooling and cracking, naturally collapsed in places.

The 'Hawaiian Gazette' for August 31, 1881, thus notified the termination of this great eruption:—

"The lava-flow which has so long been threatening Hilo may at last be regarded as at an end. In fact, it is quite impossible for it to come down again by the same channel which it has been using for the past nine months. As the support of the flowing lava in the tunnel beneath has been withdrawn, the roof has cooled, contracted, and fallen in, thus blocking up the tunnel, and also affording countless vent-holes by which the molten mass might escape, even if it could overcome the obstacles offered by the *débris* which strew its path.

"A gentleman who has given careful and scientific attention to the flow, tells us that he had followed its course for over six miles, and that for the whole length of that distance the roof had caved in, say every 150 feet or so.

"Another favourable indication of the cessation of the flow is the dense black smoke which is now rolling up from the terminal crater. This has usually been noticed at the close of former eruptions and flows. As long as the flow continues to advance, as long as the liquid lava pours out, the smoke is of a whitish colour; but as soon as it becomes black, the danger, as a rule, may be regarded as at an end."

The only remaining point of special interest to be remarked, is the condition of the crater of Kilauea, on the flank of Mauna Loa, during this tremendous activity of Mokua-wéo-wéo on its summit. It does not appear to have shown any remarkable sympathy with the latter; and I gather from the descriptions that have reached me, that it has resumed much the same appearance it presented at the time of my visit in 1879—namely, that the great north and south lakes, which ordinarily bubble and toss in a fiery flood at a depth of about 120 feet below the floor of the great crater, have all been filled up; and there have arisen peaks and cones of hard lava, that rise over 100 feet above the south bank of the great crater, which is about 1000 feet high. But there has burst forth a new opening in the great crater-floor, not far distant from the old lakes; and also a new lake, almost round in form, about 600 feet across, and lying about 70 feet below the surrounding brink.

Now the great eruption of 1881 is a story of the

THE LESSON OF FAITH AND TRUST.

past, and the people of Hilo have learnt one more lesson of faith and trust.

For ever dwelling in the midst of the sublimest sights of creation, surrounded by tremendous manifestations of every force of nature, with a wildly tempestuous sea on the one side, and on the other, a newly created earth (which they have watched from the moment when it was thrown like liquid fire from the innermost depths of the great craters, till, cooled and pulverised, and fertilised by the heavy rainfall, it has become clothed with the rich foliage of the tropics, yielding herb and fruit for the service of men), they have learnt in all these wonders of creation to recognise not merely the Divine Power (for that much was ever acknowledged by the heathen Hawaiians, when, in fear and trembling, they worshipped Pélé, the dread Fire-goddess), but rather to behold in all these glorious works the almighty hand of the Friend and Father, Whose love has never failed to encompass them with watchful care.

So day by day do they walk in the midst of the flows, fearing no evil, as those who believe that the Fire-floods will not be suffered to overwhelm them, because One, Who is the true Lord of the Fire, is ever present to shield them from its power.

THE END.

PRINTED BY WILLIAM BLACKWOOD AND SONS.

www.ingramcontent.com/pod-product-compliance
Lightning Source LLC
Chambersburg PA
CBHW032057220426
43664CB00008B/1040